# Stutterer
# Interrupted

# Stutterer Interrupted

## THE COMEDIAN WHO ALMOST DIDN'T HAPPEN

### Nina G

SHE WRITES PRESS

Published 2019
Printed in the United States of America
ISBN: 978-1-63152-642-8
ISBN: 978-1-63152-643-5
Library of Congress Control Number: 2019934127

For information, address:
She Writes Press
1569 Solano Ave #546
Berkeley, CA 94707

She Writes Press is a division of SparkPoint Studio, LLC.

*When you write a book that integrates so many parts of yourself, it is difficult to dedicate it to just one person...*

### *This book is dedicated to:*

*...my parents Kathy and Jerry, for their advocacy, for driving me to speech therapy appointments, and for sitting through hours of painfully unfunny live comedy.*

*...the Stamily, for inspiring me to become the person I always wanted to be.*

*...the memory of Michael O'Connell, who helped me bring my true self into stand-up. His comedy and his impact on the people around him will never fade.*

# Contents

# Introduction

Ask anyone who stutters and they will tell you that we are constantly interrupted. The slightest repetition or block in our speech will often result in a *$10,000 Pyramid*-style guessing match. If we stutter "p-p-p," the listener guesses everything from pizza to pumpernickel—and usually gets it wrong. If these listeners *did* actually listen, maybe the person stuttering would have a chance to finish their thought!

I have experienced interruptions my entire life. I don't just mean people talking over me. I mean my entire development as a person has been interrupted, arrested, stunted, and whatever else it says in the thesaurus. I was blessed with amazing parents and a supportive speech therapist, but nothing could shield me from the pain of growing up in a world where my voice was mocked. I remember the first time someone teased me because of my speech. I was at Wacky Waldo's, a skate shop in my hometown of Alameda, CA. I was only eight years old, but that didn't stop the owner from making fun of the way I said "bird." His mockery, however slight, signaled to me that I was different—and this was coming from a guy named Wacky Waldo.

Being treated as different was a recurring theme throughout my childhood. Teachers graded me down for "not speaking clearly," often skipping over my turn to read a prayer in class (Catholic school). It didn't help that I also had learning disabilities.

After my self-esteem was corroded all day at school, coming home and watching TV seemed like an ideal escape. But even there, in the safety of my living room, I kept receiving the message that I wasn't good enough. Television showed me images of the fluent (non-stuttering) people I was supposed to emulate, living out their perfect fictional lives in 80s sitcoms and Pepsi commercials. If someone did stutter on TV, they were either a bumbling doofus, a sociopathic killer, or a cartoon pig who walked around without pants. If I had to choose one for a role model, I guess I'd go the no-pants route.

I got the message loud and clear: I'm not normal, I'm not good enough. I took all the negative social cues and internalized them, like a box of baking soda absorbing every rotten odor in the fridge. I learned to be my own bully and shame myself. That shame continued to grow, until I was no longer in control of my life. I was determined to hide my stuttering at any cost, even my own happiness. I withdrew from all the important parts of growing up: friendships, socializing, flirting, group activities—anything that required me to speak. It wasn't enough to be interrupted by others; I was now interrupting myself. I yielded the floor to everyone (anyone) around me, because I thought my voice was defective and shouldn't be heard. I wasted years of my adult life stuck in crummy relationships because I thought I didn't deserve better. People walked over me while I worried if their feet were comfortable doing it.

Maybe you have been in a similar position. Maybe you have experienced what it's like to put yourself and your needs aside, out of fear or embarrassment. The world we live in is all too happy to crush a person's self-esteem for any reason. For me, it was stuttering and dyslexia. For someone else, it might be their body, their gender expression, their personality—any part of them that feels unloved, unaccepted and rejected. We learn to bottle up those feelings and live in hiding, disappearing deeper and deeper into our shame.

It has taken most of my life to find my way out of this trap. Truth be told, it never stops. The shame monster is always there, and I always have to be vigilant to keep him on his leash—easier said than done, especially when people are constantly reminding me of the fact that I stutter. It can be an awkward facial expression or an offhand comment. It can be someone asking if I forgot my name or if I'm having a stroke. It can be dropping whatever we are talking about and launching into a fifteen-minute lecture on the "real cause" of my stuttering, usually beginning with the phrase, "So I heard on NPR...". I've had so many strange and outrageous interactions over the years, I figured I might as well sit down and write a damn book about it.

All the stories in this book are true (certain names and details have been changed to protect people's privacy). You might read some parts and think, "There's no way someone actually said that!" I assure you, they actually said it. Some of it is hurtful. Some of it is just annoying or awkward. Over the years, I have developed my own defenses for dealing with them.

Defense number one is having empathetic friends and family. If you learn one thing in this world, learn to surround yourself with people who understand you! I have been in so many relationships where the other person accused me of overreacting whenever I relayed an incident of some mistreatment; it actually made me doubt my own feelings. Now I can ask my fluent friend Heather, "Am I overreacting?" and trust her answer. I can text my stuttering friend Gina and get her opinion on whatever is happening. I am so grateful to have people in my life who can take that weight off my shoulders. They are my rock!

Defense number two is stand-up comedy. Comedians often talk about "finding their voice as an artist." For me, it was finding my voice. Period. Comedy has given me the power to say what I want and make people listen. It has also given me hecklers who don't listen, and I'm thankful for that too. Hecklers are a safe outlet for dealing with assholes. If you tell your asshole boss to shut up, you get fired; if you tell an asshole heckler to shut up, you get applause. Thank God for hecklers! They taught me how to brush off insults and remain confident, both on and off the stage. If someone says something degrading to me one day, you can bet I'll have a roomful of strangers laughing at their stupidity a week later. Just like a best friend, comedy is able to turn my frustrations into validation.

This book is a collection of my experiences: from the self-loathing teenager who secretly dreamed of being a comedian, to the adult in crisis who finally said "fuck it" and took the plunge. Of course, my experience is just that, my experience. It is specific to me and my life as a white-Italian-American-Catholic-cis-female-heterosexual-middle-class-nonapparent-disability-having-person-et cetera. When all is said and done, I can only speak for myself—although much of what I believe is shaped by other people and their stories. Hopefully my story can inform and speak to your experience. If you stutter, if you have another disability, if you have ever felt ashamed, hopeless, or afraid because of who you are—this is for you.

## "Person Who Stutters" or Stutterer?"

This has been a contentious question in the stuttering community for decades. It is very similar to the "disabled people" versus "people with disabilities" argument.

Where I stand depends on my audience. If I am presenting to psychologists, medical doctors, speech therapists, etc., I make a point of saying "people who stutter." I want them to remember that we are more than just a diagnosis. I realize that's their job, but if they objectify our speech and forget the person attached to the stutter, it diminishes their ability to help. I know a lot of people who soured on the idea of getting professional help because their doctor/speech therapist made them feel like a bug under a microscope.

If I'm speaking to a friend, I use "person who stutters" and "stutterer" interchangeably. And since I consider you my friend, you will encounter both terms in this book. You probably noticed "STUTTERER" in big swirly letters on the cover. I don't know, *Person Who Stutters, Interrupted* just doesn't have the same ring to it. More importantly, I am proud to call myself a stutterer. Stuttering might be just one part of me, but it is a really big part. It goes beyond a disorder or a diagnosis. It goes beyond my repetitions and blocks. It connects me to a community of 70 million other people who give me strength and inspiration.

When it comes to the question of "stutterer" versus "person who stutters," I see the value in both. But that's only because of my relationship with these terms and their meanings. If you are talking to someone who stutters and the issue comes up, ask what they prefer. They may not prefer a label at all.

# 1
# Comedian Interrupted

The carpet was leopard print. The booths were a deep, modern-looking burgundy. I had just finished performing for a small audience (if a bartender and the other booked comedians count as an audience). There was also the club manager—an older woman sitting in the corner, jotting down notes to decide who would get called back for paid work. I'm pretty sure there was supposed to be a real audience that night, but since the club sold zero tickets, they could call it a closed-door audition and save face.

After the show— I mean *audition*—I walked over to the club manager and introduced myself.

"Thanks for having me," I said. "Do you have any shows where I might be a good fit?"

"You know what," she replied in a heavy Midwestern accent, "you just keep going to those open mics and one day I'm sure you'll have the confidence to stop stuttering."

I was well-versed in my options at this point. Do I smile and nod? Do I give her the finger? Do I explain the neurological underpinnings of stuttering and how they have nothing to do with confidence? Is it even worth the effort? These situations always remind me of a great bit by Dana Gould:

*Have you ever done that? Somebody says something dumb, and you calculate how long it will take to explain, and to argue, and decide instead just to agree with them and treat yourself to an ice cream sandwich?*

For people with disabilities, life is a constant question of patiently educating others or taking the proverbial ice cream sandwich. Since I was trying to get work from this lady, I chose to go through the trouble and try to change her mind. I didn't get far. Like your average dispenser of unsolicited advice, she had plenty of anecdotal evidence to support her claims: she once had a neighbor who stuttered, don't you know! Trying to bring the conversation back to "will you pay me to get on stage and tell dick jokes?" was pointless. Six months later, it was really pointless: it turns out they never got a handle on the whole selling tickets thing. The club closed down, and, despite having moderately good self-esteem, I still stutter. I should have gone the Dana Gould route and taken the damn ice cream.

That was more than six years ago. Since then I've endured hecklers, hateful YouTube comments, exclusion from comedy cliques, being told I'm "too political" for this show, being told I'm "not political enough" for that show, and everything in between. I've had bookers try to get me alone with them in my apartment (perhaps they wanted to see if my joke about stuttering and oral sex was accurate). I've met people at shows who suggested that an "intrusive brain surgery" might cure my disfluency. I've waited hours at an open mic in a laundromat to perform for two people.

Why do I continue pursuing this nightmare called stand-up comedy? Because I love it! I feel so lucky when I'm performing at the dive bar in Gilroy for no one but a strange old man who keeps showing me his chest. I feel lucky to perform at the bar in San Bruno where a fight breaks out and I have to resort to my dirtiest jokes to distract from the screaming man being dragged out in handcuffs. What other job lets you have all those experiences? To be a comedian, you have to love what you do. And I do love what I do!

Yet bringing myself to actually do it was a long and tortured process. It should have been easy: for as long as I can remember, comedy has been one of my favorite parts of being alive. My parents exposed me to Steve Martin's albums when I was four years old. In second grade, I made a sock puppet and named it Edith Ann, after the Lily Tomlin character[1]. I also had a stuffed pig, named Gilda Radner, with three little piglets velcroed to her teats: Steve Martin, Dan Aykroyd, and Bill Murray (this was during my classic Saturday Night Live phase).

I was fortunate to have access to all the classic Saturday Night Live seasons on a local UHF station. For all you millennials, UHF stations were TV channels that aired a mix of syndicated shows and cheap local programming. Weird Al even made a movie about it (featuring Emo Philips in one of his best cameos).

Speaking of Emo Philips, he was one of my favorite comics growing up. The first fan letter I ever wrote was to him, back when I was eleven years old. Imagine my excitement when he sent back an autographed headshot! A few years ago, I finally got to meet Emo at the San Francisco Punchline. He had no memory of our written exchange in the 80s, of course.

As I entered middle school and the hormones started kicking in, I didn't go for your typical Johnny Depp, New Kids on the Block teen heartthrobs. Oh no! I decorated my room with performers from *Rodney Dangerfield's Young Comedians Special* on HBO. While other girls were clipping out pictures from *Teenbeat*, I subscribed to a stand-up comedy trade paper to hunt for articles on my latest crush.

My obsession eventually metastasized into the final stage of comedy nerdom: wanting to get on stage and try it myself. Somewhere around seventh grade, I began to entertain secret fantasies of becoming a comedian. And when I say secret, I mean SECRET. Why was

I so afraid of people finding out? Self-hatred, of course! You see, I believe humor to be one of the highest forms of intelligence. In my mind, saying "I want to be a comedian," was the same as saying, "I think I'm funny and intelligent." For a special ed middle schooler with low self-esteem, that was like a thought crime.

As a closet wannabe comedian, I would sift through listings for comedy showcases and open mics in the San Francisco Guardian. I once called a bar in Oakland (Dorsey's Locker) to ask about their open mic night. The bartender answering the phone yelled out, "This bitch wants to be Eddie Murphy!" prompting some loud cackles from the bar. Embarrassed because this bitch really did want to be Eddie Murphy, I hung up without getting any information.[2]

I started writing jokes on a yellow legal pad that I stole from my mom's work. Ugh! The things I came up with! It was the worst 80s hack material you can imagine:

> *What did Ginger and Maryanne do for tampons on Gilligan's island? Did the professor make them out of coconuts?*

> *I'm Italian! I have the armpits to prove it.*

That was about as far as I got before I gave up and quit on the idea of being a comic. I didn't give up because my jokes were bad (they were). I gave up because I figured a person who stutters could never be a comedian anyway. I had no evidence to suggest otherwise. When was the last time you saw an entertainer stuttering on TV? I figured fluency had to be a requirement. So I buried my girlhood dreams and moved on.

But my love for comedy persisted. It was like the cartoon where the guy covers his mouth to sneeze and it comes out of his ears. If I couldn't pursue stand-up, my passion had to find some other outlet. When I had to write about a "great showman" for high school history, I wrote about Lorne Michaels. When I had to put together an anthology of writing for English, I wrote a paper titled "Bada Boom: An Anthology of Comedy and Humor." I even found a way to write about comedy in graduate school, with a "comparative analysis of sociocultural expressions of masculinity within the chronosystems of the Marx Brothers, Jerry Lewis and Lenny Bruce." That's the great thing about academia: you can write about anything you want as long as no one understands what the hell you're saying (did I just steal that line from Alvy Singer in *Annie Hall*?).

I finished grad school, got my doctorate in psychology, and became a frustrated dyslexic-stuttering academic. Even though I was able to complete more than eight years of college, I never felt at home in academia. I knew I had important ideas, but my learning disability made it difficult to write them out, especially in a style that felt foreign and inauthentic to who I am.

While I had doubts in my professional life, I was even more lost in my personal life. I was single for the first time in years, having recently ended a long relationship with my boyfriend-at-the-time Sean. A few months later, I met a stuttering guy named Andy. Flirting with another stutterer was so much easier. My previous interactions with men had always been tainted by a constant fear of rejection over my speech. But with Andy, I could just talk. I didn't have to worry about the way I sounded or the risk of spittle flying from my repetitive lips. Having that burden suddenly lifted made me realize how much it had been weighing me down. For the first time in my life, I didn't have to put a man behind a salad bar sneeze guard if I wanted to vamp it up!

Andy and I started dating. He lived four hours away, which made things, um, complicated. I soon learned that one of his housemates was (drumroll) a stand-up comedian! When Andy went to see his housemate perform at an open mic, I told him he should also sign up as a performer, because, "How hot would it be to see a stuttering comedian?" Andy wasn't interested. I pressed him again and again, but he had no desire to go on stage.

I was obviously projecting my own ambitions onto Andy, but it took me a while to wake up and realize it. Specifically, it took the writing of bell hooks, the feminist author who doesn't capitalize her name. Throughout her work, she talks about how women in social movements have historically shied from more prominent roles, working behind the scenes to support the male leadership. Hooks counters this with a call to action, challenging women to step into their power and enact social change. That was what I had to do! Instead of convincing some guy to live my dreams for me, I had to step up and take ownership. I thought more about that book and how it related to comedy. Dick Gregory, Paul Mooney, Lenny Bruce, Wanda Sykes—so many of my favorite comedians have used the stage to address civil rights issues. If I couldn't spread my message through academia, I would do it by bellowing dick jokes into a microphone! bell hooks, if you are reading this (for reasons I can't imagine), thank you for inspiring this stuttering white woman to follow her dream.

So now I was determined to do comedy, but I needed a place to start. Having spent most of my life in some type of education environment, the San Francisco Comedy College felt like the safest place to dip my toe. It was an actual college, in the sense that Dr. Pepper is an actual doctor, but it provided a risk-free environment to try out ideas and learn how booked shows and open mics worked. I remember driving to my first mic in San Francisco, blasting the *8 Mile* soundtrack in my Dodge Nitro. Dressed in three-inch wedge sandals and a five-dollar maternity shirt from Ross that I made work as a regular shirt, I imagined myself crushing this mic like Eminem's B-rabbit in an epic rap battle.

After waiting all night for a three-minute spot, it was finally my turn to perform. I opened with some riffing on how I drove to the show blasting Eminem in my maternity shirt, etc. The audience—a handful of tourists tricked into thinking this was a real show—couldn't have given two tenths of a shit. I shifted gears and told them a story about my friend Vanna, who stutters.

The real story goes like this: a few weeks earlier, I went to a bar with Vanna and some of her friends. There were maybe eight of us in total. Our sleazy bartender used the opportunity to flirt in bulk, taking us all on like a potential group orgy. He went down the row and asked our names, Vanna and I being last. I waited uncomfortably for our turn, knowing that one of us would stutter and inspire a dickish remark, which would have me stewing and replaying the incident for days. When it was Vanna's turn to introduce herself, she started with "V-v-v." The bartender made an unspooling "give me the rest" motion with his hand. Like a total badass, Vanna looked at him and said, "I stutter and you're going to have to wait until I finish."

I told this story to the open mic audience, but with a few key embellishments. Mimicking the bartender's "give me more" gesture, I added, "Is that what girls say when you take out your dick?" The audience laughed. My first laugh on stage! It was exhilarating. I had spent my whole life thinking of my stutter as a barrier to comedy, but it wasn't a barrier at all. It was the catalyst I needed to launch my performing career!

Looking back at it now, all my future happiness hinged on that one decision to get up on stage. I have met some of my best friends in the trenches of San Francisco comedy, an assorted gaggle of misfits baring their souls to strangers in dive bars and laundromats. Comedy put me on the path to embracing all aspects of myself, allowing me to express my ideas on my own terms and become a professional speaker. Funny how people are more impressed with "stuttering dyslexic comedian" than they are with "kinda funny unpublished academic with a doctorate," even though I'm still the same person. It's just a shift of perspective.

Shifting your perspective: that is key.

## 2
# Four Generations Disabled

Many people who stutter choose not to identify as disabled. Some feel that we don't share enough in common with people who have more apparent disabilities. Others may not want to be associated with disability because of the stigma that it carries in our culture. Personally, I view disability as a neutral characteristic. There are as many kinds of people with disabilities as there are without. An individual is an individual regardless of ability. That being said, disability can also be a source of group identity. It can be a culture and a community. For me, it has been all those things and more. It has literally been my family.

I am not the first person in my family with disabilities. I am not the second, or even the third. My father was born with hearing loss, as was his father and his father's mother. We are four generations Disabled. My great grandmother Cecilia came to the United States in the late 1916, from the Tuscany region of Italy. That's over a hundred years of blaring radios, open doors, and speaking at volumes considered loud even by Italian standards. As long as my father's bloodline has been in America, we have been Disabled.

When my father was in elementary school, the teacher sat him in the back of the classroom with a box that supposedly amplified his hearing. Although well-intentioned, this was probably the worst idea ever. Students who are Deaf or hard-of-hearing need to sit at the front of the class, because (newsflash!) it's harder to hear someone from far away. As if that weren't enough to disrupt his education, he was also constantly pulled out of class for speech therapy. He was even experimented on by doctors, who gave him radiation therapy to see if it would shrink his adenoids and cure his hearing loss.[1] It didn't work.

As a child, my dad would often sit on the curb by his house, wondering why he was born with a disability. At church, he would wait until no one was looking and drop some holy water in his ear, hoping God would miraculously grant him normal hearing. It didn't work. As he got older and learned to live with his disability, he turned his hope to the next generation, praying that none of his children would be born with hearing loss. His prayers were answered, and he got a stuttering-dyslexic daughter instead!

When I was two years old, my mom noticed something "different" about me. At an age when most children are forming words and learning to talk, I was not. I did, however, have my own language of squealing noises to indicate which foods I wanted to eat. For cheese, I made a chirping sound. Chicken, incidentally, was more of a cluck. My mom would pretend to understand what all the other noises meant, nodding her head and smiling. When I caught on that she didn't actually understand me, I got frustrated and stopped vocalizing altogether. That really worried my parents. With our family's history, they knew these were early signs of hearing loss. In fact, I did not have hearing loss. Instead I had a central auditory processing disability (CAPD). If the words you hear sound like Charlie Brown's teacher ("wa-wa-wa-wa"), as it does in CAPD, the words out of your mouth are also going to be "wa-wa-wa-wa-wa."

My parents took me to the doctor to test my hearing. When the tests came back in normal range, they enrolled me in speech therapy at the Oakland Children's Hospital. There I was seen by a woman named Elaine for speech articulation issues.

Elaine Wells was the first, last, and best speech therapist I ever had. I don't remember loving therapy, but I do remember loving Elaine. She had a Dorothy Hamill hairstyle and pictures of her children all over her office. She worked with me on my Rs, Ss, and Ts. She taught me how to keep my tongue in my mouth. She made me practice talking with Cheerios in my mouth (I recall being disappointed that they weren't Lucky Charms). All the sessions were free, paid with a grant scholarship to the hospital. Eventually, I had to be transferred to another speech therapist in Alameda. He smelled like cigarettes and had yellow teeth. I wouldn't get to see Elaine again until I was in middle school.

By the time my articulation issues improved, I began to stutter and have difficulty reading. This was in third grade, when impaired reading starts to affect all areas of education. I was no longer learning to read, but reading to learn, which meant I couldn't keep up with the lessons in class. My teacher spoke with my parents about the possibility of dyslexia.

For the rest of that year—and many years after—my parents had to fight for my education. Teachers and administrators resisted them at every turn, saying I wasn't good enough for their school, that I was robbing an enrollment slot from smarter, more deserving children. They straight up told my mom and dad that I wouldn't be capable of more than flipping burgers as an adult.

My parents weren't about to let some narrow-minded Catholic school dictate my future. My mom contacted U.C. Berkeley to find out what happens when students with learning disabilities go to college. The university wrote her back with a description of all the services and accommodations they provide—services and accommodations I was definitely NOT getting at my school. My mom presented the letter to my principal and teachers, to prove that a student can meet academic standards while still receiving accommodations for their disability. My teachers were unimpressed. They doubted I would ever finish high school, much less get into a university like Berkeley. Nonetheless, the letter was saved in a drawer at home with other important documents, like my social security card and savings bonds from my First Communion.

As much as Catholic school sucked, I was lucky to have a family like mine. My parents were way ahead of the curve when it came to caring for a child with disabilities. My dad had his experience with hearing loss, and my mom had seen her mother live with the effects of post-polio syndrome. I wasn't the "special" one; disability was the family status quo. It was just another thing you dealt with, like flossing or doing taxes. It didn't define you or limit your choices in life. You could work, marry, have kids. My parents knew this from seeing their own parents live normal lives, and they had similar expectations of me. If my teachers said I couldn't achieve the same things as other students, my parents let me know those teachers were full of shit. In a house where Richard Pryor specials were considered family entertainment, they may have actually used those exact words.

When my dad was growing up, his father drove him long distances to get the best possible help for his hearing loss. Going the extra mile (or many miles) for children with disabilities is a tradition in our family. Between his day job and night job, my dad would drive me forty miles to see Elaine. By the time we got there, he was so exhausted that he usually slept in the waiting room. Once, after waking him up, Elaine said, "You know, Jerry, there are other speech therapists closer to you." He replied, "Yeah, but Nina likes you." The tradition has continued to the next generation. When my niece was diagnosed with a learning disability, you can bet we were all there at the school meetings, making sure she got the best accommodation plan possible.

Caring for children with disabilities goes beyond making sure they get the right accommodations and treatment. I still stutter and have dyslexia, and all the therapy in the world isn't going to change that. But my parents showed me how to accept these things, even if that acceptance is a lifelong process. When I was in sixth grade, my dad coached the Catholic Youth Organization (CYO) girls' softball team. At the beginning of our first practice, he announced, "I'm deaf and you're just going to have to speak up when you're talking to me."

I was horrified to see him present his disability out in the open. I waited for the other girls to laugh. They didn't laugh. In fact, they didn't care at all. My father wasn't ashamed of his disability, nor was he ashamed of mine. We were just there to throw a ball in the grass and have a good time. Now, when I do stand-up, public speaking, and even job interviews, I like to tell my audience, "I stutter and you're just going to have to wait patiently for all my brilliant ideas." I guess the apple didn't fall far from the tree.

Of course, not all parents of children with disabilities have disabilities themselves, but they can still serve as role models. There are going to be peers, teachers, and random passersby who make children feel bad about themselves. Our job is to protect them, to make them feel both special and normal at the same time. If that sounds tricky, it is. Being a good role model doesn't mean being perfect; my dad once lost his temper and threw an eraser across the room because my brother was being difficult with his drafting homework (we still laugh about it today). What's important is being authentic and promoting the values we want our children to believe in. It is ultimately up to the person with disabilities to decide who they are and how they want to be treated. Which is also tricky. Look how hard it's been for me!

# 3

# I, Nina

When I was in sixth grade, I decided to run for student government. To be more precise, I ran for "religious affairs officer" (Catholic school government has no separation of church and state, naturally). Duties of the religious affairs officer included collecting mission money and saying the morning prayer at assembly. I just wanted an excuse to get out of class. For me and my dyslexia, any time not in the classroom was a good time. I wasn't worried about the morning prayer, since it's easier not to stutter when reciting a passage or speaking in unison with a group. What was not to love about this job?

I constructed my campaign speech to exclude any words that might trip me up. I practiced my speech over and over, until it became another rote passage I could recite like the morning prayer. The only downside to reciting my speech on autopilot[1] was that it took away any emotion or authenticity. Then again, I wasn't exactly emotional about selling candy bars for Jesus. If I could just get through this one speech, it would be smooth sailing from here on out. Or so I thought.

I won the election, despite my opponent claiming that I bribed the grammar school kids by handing out Tootsie Roll Pops with my name on them. You call it bribery; I call it cross-promotion. Dirty Catholic school politics always triumph!

The new student council was to be sworn in at the beginning of the next school year. In true Catholic fashion, the school did this with an overly elaborate ceremony. When I found out I would have to give an inauguration speech, I felt my stomach twist. After agonizing over that last speech, I was back to square one! Worse than square one, because this time we had to rehearse the ceremony as a group. No more practicing alone in my room until I had worked out all the "stutter bugs;" this time my peers were going to see how the sausage gets made.

My teacher, Mrs. Castillo, led us through the rehearsal. Even though it was the 80s, Mrs. Castillo dressed about two or three decades behind. She looked like the female villain from a Frankie and Annette beach party movie. Between her cat-eyed glasses, polyester suit, and beehive hairdo, Mrs. Castillo looked like she was living in an alternate timeline where rock music is illegal and married part-ners sleep in matching twin beds. I remember once staring at her during a windy lunchtime recess. Garbage and leaves were blowing everywhere, but the wind couldn't penetrate her dyed-black bouffant. Not a single hair out of place!

As we rehearsed the ceremony, I learned that each student had to state, "I, [insert name here]" before reading the inaugural oath. Saying one's name is often a stumbling block for people who stutter. For me, the combination of saying "I" followed by "Nina" is a guar-anteed stutterpalooza. We can contrive sentences to avoid problem words all day long, but there's no substitute for your name unless you straight up change it, which some of us might do from time to time. But this wasn't a Starbucks order where I can be sly and say my name is Enid. I had to say "I, Nina G..."

I stuttered in the rehearsal, drawing laughs from the seventh and eighth graders who had been elected for their "leadership qualities." What really pisses me off is that one of the girls laughing had a mild stutter herself. Thanks a lot, Elizabeth! I guess there's no such thing as stuttering solidarity in the dog-eat-dog world of middle school. Mrs. Castillo attempted to intervene by telling the students to "shut up," but it didn't work. I left feeling defeated. I also left with the realization that Mrs. Castillo was actually kind of cool.

At least one of my peers didn't laugh. He was an eighth grader, a little on the hyperactive side (I've always gotten along with hyperactive males, which is a plus when you work in comedy). I don't remember his name. I used to call him Elvis, because one year he dressed like a 1970s Elvis in a white jumpsuit for Halloween—just the type of confident weirdness I like!

After the inauguration rehearsal, Elvis approached me and asked, "Can you say ninja? Because if you can say ninja, you just switch it over to Nina instead." Although I'm usually annoyed by free advice on stuttering, this was thoughtful stuff by eighth-grade-boy standards (plus, he was kind of cute). Elvis was offering to be my ally when no one else would. Because of him, I didn't feel completely alone during one of the most humiliating moments in my preteen life.

I spent the rest of the week practicing my name. I practiced alone in my room. I practiced in front of my parents. I practiced during speech therapy with Elaine. My parents were usually okay with me playing hooky, but they never mentioned it as an option for inauguration day. I guess they didn't want me running away from my problems (unless, of course, that problem was school hours conflicting with matinee prices for the new Steve Martin movie).

When the big day arrived, I was so focused on my own name that I couldn't think of anything else. I, Nina. I, Nina. You, Nina! You can do this!

We, the elected student officials, took our seats on stage, the girls crossing their legs at the ankle as instructed. The principal, Mrs. Castillo, Sister Theresa, and Father Dow sat across from us. The entire school was there, along with some parents and a journalist from the Alameda Time Star (I guess it was a slow news day). With all the fanfare the school was making, you'd think they were inaugurating John F. Kennedy in that auditorium.

Father Dow began the ceremony with a prayer. Then it was our turn. One by one, the student officials began stating their names. "I, Susan Quigley." "I, Brian Hansen." Again and again, I mentally practiced my speech techniques. I walked to the podium and said my name.

"I, N-n-N-n-Nina."

In my seventh-grade-girl mind, my life was over. That was it! I would need to transfer schools, maybe even move. Everyone knew about my stutter now—even the Time Star! I could already picture tomorrow's headline: "Girl Stutters in Front of Entire School, Disgraces Hometown." This was before we had websites like Upworthy to turn other people's trauma into inspirational clickbait: "This Brave Girl Stuttered in Front of Her Entire School. You Won't Believe What Happened Next!"

What happened next was me sulking off the stage, bracing for the same derisive laughter I got in rehearsal—only this time from an entire auditorium, packed with hundreds of people. I walked back to my seat, expecting the jeers to begin any second. A girl in my class, Sara, turned to me and whispered, "Nina! Good job!" At first I thought she was being sarcastic, but no, she really meant it. Really? Good job? I was shocked by this rare example of middle school empathy.[2]

I went on with the rest of my day, waiting for the hammer to drop. If my peers hadn't ripped me apart in assembly, surely they would at recess. If school is a prison, then recess is the exercise yard where the shanking happens. I was a dead girl walking. I spent recess talking to Elvis, who felt like the safest person to be around. That was when a snotty second grade boy approached us. He walked up to me and said, "Hey, N-N-Nina," hoping to impress the big kids with his wit. Elvis was not impressed. He gently kneeled down, looking the second grader straight in the eye. "If I hear you say anything like that again, I'm going to tell everyone that your penis is this big," he said, indicating half an inch with his thumb and forefinger. Devastating stuff for an eight-year-old.

It was, as far as I can remember, the first time someone other than my parents stood up for me. None of my other friends would stick their neck out like that—especially in middle school, where everyone is afraid of the herd turning on them. It was truly an exceptional moment in the life of a seventh grade girl. I remember thinking, "This is the nicest thing anyone has ever done for me!"

And how does a seventh grade girl process a traumatic-turned-heroic event like this? She has a crush on her hero for the rest of the year. And, full disclosure, she might even try to track him down on Facebook twenty-something years later, when she is single and in her thirties.

Besides discovering my latest crush, I learned some important things that day. Lesson number one: I could stutter in public and survive. Until then, I thought I had to be fluent in order to participate in anything. Self-esteem issues continued to plague me, but being able to stutter in front of everyone and walk away unscathed was a watershed moment. It must have been difficult for my parents to let me participate in that ceremony, knowing how much terror and potential trauma it could cause. I'm glad they did. I'm grateful to have lived that experience.

The second thing I learned was that I had allies outside of my family and speech therapists. I could put emotional trust in my peers (at least some of them) and count on their support. It's a great feeling when you know someone has your back, especially if that someone has more power—like an eighth grader when you're a seventh grader, or a boy when you're a girl in the 1980s (it's a shitty fact that people feel more comfortable messing with women than with men, so it never hurts to have backup from a male ally). Ever since the Elvis incident, I have tried to surround myself with people who stand by and support me—although I've still duped myself into plenty of relationships that provide neither.

The last and final lesson I learned that day relates to comedy. Simply put, if ANYONE makes fun of me, I do what Elvis did: I make fun of them back! Ideally with a comment about their actual or metaphorical penis, if applicable. I'm sorry if you were expecting this chapter to end on something heartwarming or inspirational, but a good comedian always ends on a dick joke.

# 4
# Too Weird for Prom

"**Y**ou are so weird."

Those were the words of Justin, the first boy who tried to kiss me.

I was sixteen years old. Justin and I had spent the afternoon driving in my hella cool yellow and green 1954 Chevy Sports Coupe (the culmination of two years working at my Auntie Norma's daycare center). We drove to the old UC Theater in Berkeley to see a movie, something pseudo-intellectual that proved how smart and sophisticated we were. We ended up bored off our asses, being at that age when your frontal lobe is trying to grasp a work of art but really just wants to laugh at fart jokes.

We decided to go back to my place and watch *Manhattan*, the 1979 Woody Allen classic. With my parents out of the house and the two of us sitting on my bedroom floor, I guess he thought something was going to happen. Somewhere around the part of the movie where Woody and Diane Keaton get caught in the rain, Justin made his move. He gently tilted my head to meet his gaze and said, "Nina, you are the sweetest girl I ever met."

Even at sixteen, I knew he was full of shit! *Sweetest ever?* Based on what, two dates and some awkward flirting in the hallway between classes? Other girls might have fallen for that shtick, but not me. I mean, sure, he was kind of cute and part of me did want to kiss him…

I don't even want to say what happened next, it's so embarrassing. But good writing is about authenticity, so…here it goes.

He looked into my eyes and waited for something to happen. That's when I yelled, "HEADBUTT!" and slammed our foreheads together. I don't know why I did it. I guess I thought it would be a funny way to diffuse the situation, because first kisses need to be diffused, right? Maybe I was trying to turn real life into a scene from a comedy, because that's my comfort zone (I think I was trying to channel the date scene in *The Jerk*). I mean, if it had happened organically, I might have licked the side of his face like Navin Johnson (if you don't get that reference, please drop this book on the floor and go watch *The Jerk* immediately!).

Needless to say, real life isn't a Steve Martin comedy. Unlike Bernadette Peters, Justin was not charmed by my oddball antics. His droopy kissy eyes jolted open and he stared at me in shock. "You are so weird," he said. I went from "sweetest ever" to "so weird" in two seconds. That's a pretty short "ever."

After attacking this hormonal teenage boy with my skull, I could tell he was annoyed. I took him home in my still hella cool 1954 Chevy Sports Coupe and we said our goodbyes. The relationship quickly deteriorated, to the point where we didn't even greet each other in the hallway. This became a repeating pattern for all my future attempts at romance. My goofy sense of humor, combined with weird behaviors to hide my stuttering, almost always sabotaged the relationship.

Part of it is just who I am. I'm more comfortable with first kisses that are rooted in nonsense. The first time I kissed Ethan, my husband, we were watching *Love and Death* (yes, another Woody Allen film). Maybe my subconscious was going for a successful reboot of the Justin date. What's the psychobabble word for it… corrective experience!

So why did I headbutt a boy who was trying to kiss me? There are a few reasons. One reason is that sexual abuse occurred in my extended family. It was never properly dealt with, and many in the family tried to keep it a secret. Fearing for my safety, my mother made a point of teaching me to ward off sexual assault. I guess you could say she was too successful. My self-defense reflex kept me safe from touchy-feely relatives, but it also generalized to medical doctors, dentists, and future boyfriends/love interests. It prevented me from enjoying intimacy without being suspicious of a man's motives or my own physical urges. My mom did the right thing by keeping me safe; it just sucks that I had to worry about that kind of thing, especially at such a young age.

The other reason for the headbutt was my stuttering. I know, by now you're thinking I could blame global warming on stuttering, but hear me out. Erratic behaviors (like headbutts) were all part of the character I played to hide my stutter. Sometime during middle school, I discovered that acting weird made me stutter less. By using unnatural intonations, pauses, and funny voices, I could bypass the brain pathway that caused me to stutter. If anyone asked why I was acting strange, I didn't need to explain—I was the "weird kid." Somehow that seemed better than being the "stuttering kid."

Now I can hear you saying . . . wait. Back up, Nina. You can bypass the part of your brain that causes stuttering? By doing a funny voice? That's right! Look at Marilyn Monroe. She was a stutterer,[1] did you know that? Probably not, because she hid it by talking in her fake sexy voice. Some lifehack, huh? The trick works because stuttering is thought to originate from somewhere in the left side of the brain, near the area that produces speech. Meanwhile, on the right side of the brain, you have the areas that produce the functions of intonation or singing. When a stutterer uses this side of their brain as the predominate function of expression, they don't stutter. This explains why Bill Withers and Mel Tillis stutter when they talk, but not when they sing. It also explains why I could successfully prank call my friends by using a fake voice (at least before caller ID).

Once I realized that I could achieve fluency by playing the weird kid, it was a hard habit to break. I was already a little weird to begin with, so it didn't feel entirely unnatural. Even if I was a less authentic version of myself, I was still "myself." It is not unusual for young people with non-apparent disabilities to mask their insecurities with abberant behavior. As they learn to conceal the disability, their behavior is simply labeled as "acting out" or "troublemaking." And that's the whole point. If you're an insecure teenager, which one seems more attractive: the bad kid who skips homework because they're a rebel, or the kid with learning disabilities who can't do the homework because they need accommodations? Following this line of thinking, I came to the conclusion that it was better to be seen as troubled than dumb.

I was never the class clown; you need a certain degree of confidence to pull that off. I was more like the class quiet-kid in the back, only interested in making myself laugh. I made fun of the other kids, messed with boys I had crushes on, and generally refused to act like the other girls. Instead of joining in the adolescent gossip of my peers (and risking a stutter), I invented other ways to amuse myself.

Once, while eating French fries, I found an unopened maxi-pad sitting near a garbage can. To everyone else it was a discarded feminine hygiene product; to me it was a blank canvas of infinite possibilities. I took the ketchup packet from my fries and painted my masterpiece. When the work was finished, I stuck it on the wall for everyone to admire. I stood and watched the reactions of everyone in the school, an endless flow of disgusted and confused faces passing by. It was better than the Macy's Thanksgiving Day parade. If only YouTube had existed back then, I'd probably be up to a million views by now!

So yes, I definitely earned my reputation as the weird kid. This extended to my interactions with the opposite sex. I remember this one boy, Dan. I sorta had a crush on him, but I was more interested in getting back at him for teasing me in English and murdering my imaginary egg-baby (you know, one of those "pretend to be an adult" assignments). One day we arrived at school early and were hanging out before first period. I don't remember how it happened, but things quickly escalated until I was serenading Dan with a gender-modified version of Biz Markie's *You Got What I Need*:

> *You, you got what I need, but you say she's just a friend*
> *And you say she's just a friend, oh baby...*

Dan's Irish complexion lit up bright red. His face literally matched the color of his 1980s skater hair. It was so noticeable that our teacher, Mr. Dare, even commented on it. "Dan's not as red as the love I have for him," I chimed in, heading to class before the bell rang. Dan's friend, Ray, ran after me. I thought he was going to confront me for embarassing his friend. Instead, he gave me Dan's class schedule so I could follow him around and heckle him all day. Apparently high school friendship is worth less than the cheap thrill of Schadenfreude.

As much as these memories amuse me, they were (surprisingly enough) not conducive to a healthy social development. My behavior alienated me from potential friendships and boyfriends. My interests were never age-appropriate (I was the only girl in school with a Lenny Bruce record collection). There were other kids with learning disabilities and other kids who stuttered, but God forbid we should ever talk about it openly with each other. There was no one for me to fit in with, not even the angsty mod kids. I remember my mom picking me up from school and commenting on all the "weirdos" with their dyed hair and black lipstick. If only she knew I was considered the weird one, even by their standards. You know you might be an outcast when someone who looks like Marilyn Manson calls you a freak.

In junior year, I had a crush on a boy named Eric. He was cute, but in a quiet, gangly kind of way that made him seem accessible.

Eric's best friend, on the other hand, was a dick. He was short and mean—your typical Napoleon complex. He would always tease and belittle me, no doubt because it made him feel bigger. One day he told my friend, "Eric would probably ask Nina to the prom, but she's so weird!" That really stung. Why my best friend thought I should hear this is still a mystery to me.

I ended up spending prom night alone, watching Saturday Night Live. That night they aired one of my all-time favorite sketches, in which Mike Meyers plays the host of a fictional West German TV show called "Sprockets." Meyers' character is a pretentious, ultra-modern dada type who shouts random phrases like "Touch my monkey!" Then Phil Hartman shows up and starts screaming fake German gibberish while everyone does robotic dance moves to bad 80s Eurobeat. I laughed so hard that I forgot all about prom. I immediately sent a fan letter to Mike Meyers, telling him how much I loved Sprockets—although, I added, *Wayne's World* would probably be the sketch that made him famous. This was before he was even a steady cast member. Meyers wrote back with an autographed headshot. Two years later, *Wayne's World* became one of the most iconic films of the 90s. Getting Mike Meyers' autograph and proving my comedy psychic powers was probably more gratifying than drinking Kool-Aid from a ladle and awkwardly shuffling around a darkened basketball court. But then again, I'll never know.

I didn't really come out of my shell until I was in my thirties. Better late than never, I guess! I owe it all to the stuttering community. Meeting friendly, authentic people who stutter showed me that I could just be myself, without making weirdness my primary characteristic. Don't get me wrong, I'm still weird, but now that part of me is better integrated into my overall identity. I mean, if the opportunity ever presented itself, I would still do the Maxi-pad ketchup stunt. Because it's hilarious. Just remind me to film it next time, because it's totally going viral.

# 5

# How Howard Stern Taught Me Hope and Self-acceptance (Yes, Howard Stern)

The name on my Safeway Club Card is "Nina Bababooey." I get a little thrill every time I swipe my card and the cashier says, "Thank you, Ms. Bababooey…"

I once went to a taping of *America's Got Talent*. But I didn't go to see a talent show…

Before the taping started, I stood up and started shouting "F Jackie! Four inches is fine!" at the top of my lungs…

Alright, I'm just going to come out and say it: I'm a huge Howard Stern fan!

*No, Nina, noooo! How can you call yourself a Disabled feminist and support that awful man?*

I realize that not everyone is a fan of Howard Stern. That's fine; I get it. In my case, I became a fan for very personal reasons. And those reasons are tangled up in a lifetime of tension between me, the media, and disability.

I was nine years old when I first saw another person stutter. My dad was in the living room watching football. Suddenly, I heard him shout, "Nina, come look at the TV!" Reporters were interviewing Oakland Raiders cornerback Lester Hayes, and he was stuttering. Instead of feeling pride, I projected my own insecurities. "Everyone is going to make fun of him," I thought. Imagine my surprise when I went to school the next day and no one cared. I guess people give you a free pass when you're catching interceptions for the home team.

As cool as it was to see someone stutter on TV, there wasn't much about Lester Hayes that I could relate to. I never cared much about sports, even though I grew up in a Raider Nation household. I could never figure out how to emotionally invest in 22 men fighting over a piece of rubber. I still wear my Lester Hayes jersey though.

Another stuttering celeb from my childhood was country singer Mel Tillis. Although I've come to appreciate his music with age, Mel Tillis was not someone I could relate to as a child (no matter how many times I saw *Cannonball Run*). Like I said before, the closest thing I had to a role model at the time was Porky Pig.

All that changed when I was fifteen. I was watching an obscure, low-budget TV show hosted by a weird looking guy with wannabe-rocker hair. He would say obnoxious things and parade women around like sex objects. He also made me laugh with some really funny bits. That man, of course, was Howard Stern. But the person who really caught my eye was a member of Stern's supporting cast, a man they called "Stuttering John." Stuttering John was exactly that, a guy named John who stuttered.[1] Howard would send John into press conferences and red carpet events, where he would ambush celebrities with horrible and inappropriate questions. It was hard to tell how much of their discomfort was from his questions and how much was from his stuttering. I took morbid interest in parsing their disgusted reactions, something I knew all too well from my own experience. But I had never seen that experience reflected on TV before.

Howard and the other show-regulars would sometimes make fun of John's stuttering, but it didn't feel like he was a victim. It felt like inclusion. If Howard Stern makes small dick jokes about himself, teases Gary "Baba Booey" Dell'abate for his big teeth, and mocks literally everyone else on the show, it would be discrimination *not* to make fun of Stuttering John. It sounds strange, but watching a stutterer get teased by his friends was more empowering for me than seeing a respected musician or star athlete who stutters. But then I wasn't a sports fan or a country music fan. I was a comedy fan. Stuttering John was stuttering in my language.

Unlike the disabled characters who only appear for "a very special episode" of a sitcom, Stuttering John was a regular cast member. Every week I could look forward to seeing someone on TV who talked like me. This is how I learned hope and self-acceptance from Howard Stern. He presented a reality where you could be dysfluent and it was okay. In fact, it was more than okay. Stuttering John's differences made him a celebrated member of this dysfunctional family. He was part of the joke but also in on the joke, a secret agent of Howard's underground versus the sacred cows of Hollywood. I remember when Chevy Chase made a snide joke about punching Stuttering John to cure his stutter. That was the day I started hating Chevy Chase. I don't care if *National Lampoon's Vacation* is a great movie. You are on my shit list, Chevy—if that is your real name (it's not).

After introducing me to my first stuttering TV role model, Howard Stern introduced me to another first: a stuttering woman on TV. Her name was also Nina! She wore a bikini and sold hot dogs on the side of the road, because, you know, Howard Stern. It might not be PC, but when was the last time you saw a woman stutter on TV? Like, ever? If stuttering is represented, it's almost always by white men. It's like TV executives think people's heads will explode if a character embodies more than one token trait: Gay, black, AND disabled?

KA-BOOM! *Glee* almost gave us an Asian American female who stutters, but, in a remarkably stupid plot twist, it turned out that her character was only pretending to stutter (*Glee* producers and writers, you are also on my shit list)! So yeah, seeing Nina the sexy hot dog vendor was a big deal for me. There was misinformation in her interview, like Howard saying that stuttering is a psychological trait (it's neurological). Even if he didn't have his facts straight, I appreciate that Howard was willing to depict a real person whom "polite society" would rather pretend didn't exist. To me, that is more progressive than any sterilized, non-offensive representation of diversity that you'll find in the media today.

Still, many people associate Howard Stern with sexism, ableism, chauvinism, and every other "ism" you wouldn't want attached to your name. They hear bits of stories, snippets of quotes, and let that become their perception. Part of this is Howard's own doing. He attracts and embraces controversy. He is one of those rare public figures to spark protests from both the left and the right. It has become part of his brand, a source of hype to draw in new listeners. But once you sit down and listen, the product proves far less sensational than the marketing: it turns out that Howard Stern is a reasonable, thoughtful human being!

Regarding sexism on the show, it seems to have been a product of its time. Howard's shock jock persona from the 80s would be sexist by today's standards, but he is no longer the same person or the same performer. If society can change its standards over time, so can artists and entertainers. There are still sexist characters on *The Howard Stern Show*, but now they appear in an admonitory context. Ronnie the Limo Driver will objectify women and get criticized and humiliated as a result. Then there's the fact that Howard Stern is constantly bringing female comedians onto his show. That might not sound like a big deal for those who don't follow the industry, but when late night producers are caught whispering that "women aren't funny," it makes you appreciate Howard's no-bullshit approach to booking women. He's not doing it to virtue signal, which is probably impossible for someone with his reputation anyway. His only goal seems to be meeting real and interesting people.

As for ableism on the show, it's true that Howard Stern makes fun of people with disabilities. He makes fun of all his guests. By not putting on the kid gloves for disabled guests, he is signaling that they are like everyone else. He invites them back on the show, and, over time, gets to know them as individuals. They are allowed to be themselves. They can be sexual. They can be assholes. They can be more than just calculated images of Forrest Gump inspiration for the masses.

Over the years, I have watched Howard and his crew change from their exposure to people with disabilities. They acknowledge the language of the disability community and even use it in their own vernacular. This is not lost on listeners. I have personally experienced the benefit of Howard Stern's impact on attitudes toward disability. When someone comes up to me after a show and says, "Excuse me, can I ask you a personal question?" I instinctively clench up and prepare for the worst—unsolicited advice, or an unwelcome comment. But every now and then, the question will be, "Have you thought about contacting *The Howard Stern Show*?" When that happens, I know I've made a new friend.

I don't speak for everyone in the stuttering or disability community. Some might be offended when Howard makes fun of Stuttering John. Of course, I don't condone making fun of people who stutter. But when certain individuals have genuine love for each other—especially comedians—teasing can be another way of showing affection.[2] People who stutter are just people, and there are all kinds of people. Some bond through crude humor and verbal roughhousing. Others are more mellow and sensitive. How a person expresses love and respect within their tribe is up to them.

As a comedian who deals in dick jokes and F-bombs, I have a tribe of close friends who are free to mock me all they want (and I am free to mock them back, with a vengeance). The traditional roast is one of the highest honors that a comedian can receive. If someone asks you to be on their roast panel, it means you have earned that person's love and respect. They are trusting you to handle their ego in one of the most vulnerable settings possible. There is a similar under-standing among me and my comedy friends. Once we have passed the threshold of mutual love, we have earned the right to make fun of each other. Mutual teasing that doesn't degrade or hold power over someone is acceptable—as long as it's funny! But if we aren't friends and you make fun of me or my speech, you better watch yourself! You will end up on my shit list somewhere between Chevy Chase and the producers of *Glee*.

So that's the story of how and why I became a Howard Stern fan. As a woman who stutters, it would be nice to identify with people on TV besides a bikini babe selling hot dogs on the side of the road, but so far there haven't been many contenders. And when a disabled feminist says the only place she saw herself reflected on TV was *The Howard Stern Show*, you know the media needs to get its shit together.

# 6
# Ch-Ch-Changes

It was the summer of 1990. I was sixteen. I sat alone in the blue glow of the living room, eyes fixed on yet another episode of *Late Night with David Letterman*. Dave teased the next segment and went to a commercial break, as I settled in the couch resigning myself to another wave of ads. Come see Paul at the Diamond Center! Now open in San Jose! I'm George Zimmer from the Men's Warehouse. You're going to like the way you look… I guarantee it. Then another commercial came on. It was for the National Stuttering Project (NSP) in San Francisco. I don't remember anything about the actual ad, but I remember seeing it and feeling like my life was about to change. And it was.

A few days later, I went to the NSP office in San Francisco to get involved in any way I could. I ended up working as a volunteer in the mailroom. Okay, so there was no actual mailroom *per se*, but I spent every day stuffing envelopes, folding newsletters, and licking stamps, reporting directly to the executive director, John Ahlbach. As I got to know him better, I found out that John worked as a high school teacher. This was a big deal for me, as I was considering a similar career at the time.

I had given serious thought to becoming a third grade teacher.

31

Third grade marked the most painful year of my childhood, when I was diagnosed with a learning disability and my stuttering became more apparent. It was the year when my teacher told my parents that I wasn't smart enough and didn't belong in the school due to my disabilities. If I became a third grade teacher, I thought, maybe I could spare other kids from going through that kind of trauma.[1] But then, much like comedy, I thought teaching was an off-limits profession for people who stutter. Meeting John changed all that. If he could stutter and become a teacher, so could I! My future was no longer uncharted territory; someone had already been there and made a life of it.

Seeing your experiences reflected in positive role models is an important part of any community (especially for minority groups). Unfortunately, many examples of successful people who stutter don't really stutter at all—at least not in public. Let me put it this way: have you ever heard Joe Biden or James Earl Jones speak? Do you think of them as people who stutter? Making them the primary role models for children who stutter is like saying, "You can be successful too, all you have to do is stop stuttering!" Instead of feeling good about yourself, you look at these people and wonder what you're doing wrong. You wonder why you can't fix your voice and get a job as Vice President or Darth Vader.

We need to show children that there are all kinds of people who stutter: comedians, military personnel, salespeople, sports journalists—people of all ages, genders, and cultures. Volunteering with the NSP exposed me to all kinds of people who stutter, and it did wonders for my self-esteem. I was surrounded by well-adjusted adults who could speak without fluency and still lead normal lives. They weren't held back or forced into hiding. And if they were normal, that meant I was normal too!

When that summer ended, I went into senior year determined to be myself and not hide behind the "weird kid" persona. I spoke in my natural voice and started making peace with my repetitions and blocks. I remember my friend Mike seeing my NSP membership card and asking what it was. I smiled and told him it was my "license to stutter." It really was. Having achieved a new level of self-acceptance, I became a more integrated person. Unfortunately, by senior year, it's a little late to change your reputation, no matter what 80s teen movies would have you believe. Despite my newfound confidence, I was still considered "too weird" for prom.

After graduation, I spent the summer doing more volunteer work for the NSP. This time I got to work at their annual conference, which was held in San Francisco that year. I had never seen so many people who stutter in all my life! I helped attendees check in. I learned to make eye contact when they stuttered on their names. I saw how powerful it was to be able to stutter without interruption. While I found solace in being around people who talked like me, there weren't many women my age—or any age, for that matter. As a teenage girl outnumbered by older men, I wasn't able to get comfortable and fully enjoy the event. Like a middle school dance, I observed my surroundings with little interaction.

When the summer ended and I started college, I became overwhelmed with schoolwork and quickly forgot about stuttering communities and conventions. It would be ten whole years before I dipped my toe back into the waters of the Stuttering community again. But that's a story for another time.

# 7

# Stuttering in Grad School

Thanks to my experience with the NSP, I went into college feeling more comfortable with myself than ever before. In theory, this should have improved my social life. In theory. By the time I arrived at UC Berkeley (after two years of community college), I was so overwhelmed with schoolwork that I didn't have time for a social life. I was determined to earn my B.A. in psychology within four years, despite the fact that I needed several semesters of remedial courses on top of the normal workload. Combine that with dyslexia and you have a recipe for zero free time. While my peers were out having fun and developing interpersonal skills, I was alone in a library reviewing textbooks and flashcards. In hindsight, maybe I should have eased up on the studying and focused more on integrating myself as a person. I needed to go to parties, go on dates, and fully experience life in my twenties, like the other students.

Except I wasn't like the other students. I was under enormous pressure to prove myself. My teachers had doubted me since the third grade, and I still carried those doubts inside of me. I often wondered, "Do I really belong here?" I mean, I had a learning disability in a place of higher learning! Not to mention the fact that no one in my family had ever finished college. I didn't come from this world. I felt like an outsider.

I was able to pay my way through undergrad with financial assistance from the Department of Rehabilitation. My parents supported me Italian style, i.e. letting me live in their house and eat their food. For those of you keeping score, you can add "commutes from home" to the list of ways Nina didn't fit in with the other kids at Berkeley. Part of the distance I felt from my peers was the actual distance I drove every morning in my 1954 Chevy hooptie (and sometimes my dad's Geo Prism). When the day was done, they would head back to the dorms for co-ed revels, and I would head back to Alameda.

Graduate school was different. After missing out on dating as an undergrad, I forced myself to make time for it now. I went out with a guy who worked at the library (where else was I going to meet someone?). It didn't last. I joined a softball team with some other psychology students and ended up dating one of them. It didn't last. I dated a guy I met swing dancing (that's what young singles did in the 90s, believe it or not). It didn't last. I dated a guy who helped me create a website for my dissertation. Do you think it lasted? I used to joke that all my relationships came with a six-month expiration date.

In addition to dating, another new feature of grad school was student loans. Every semester added to the mounting financial pressure, and I had to graduate on time if I didn't want to drown in debt. So I worked my ass off. Almost every minute of every day was dedicated to reading, writing, studying, or thinking about reading, writing, and studying. I somehow found time to also work at my Auntie Norma's daycare center, earning what I could to offset some of that student debt. Juggling school, romance, and a part-time job was enough to make my head explode. My mom eased the pressure by making sure I didn't have to develop any independent living skills, like doing laundry and cooking. That's right, I was still living in Italian-American subsidized housing, A.K.A. my parents' place (if someone kicks their adult children out of the house, you can bet they don't have a vowel at the end of their name).

Even though I was devoting every second of my life to school, I never got comfortable in academia. I knew I had important ideas, but my learning disability made it difficult to write them out, especially in a style that felt inauthentic to who I am. My first instinct in communication usually involves an F-bomb (early exposure to Richard Pryor will do that), so I had to do a lot of translating in my head. If I spoke unfiltered, God help us all. In one of my first graduate courses, we were learning how Sigmund Freud covered up cases of sexual abuse with his female clients. Naturally, this made me angry, so I blurted out the first words that popped into my head: "FREUD HELLA SUCKS!" The class erupted into giggles. Of course it was easier for them to laugh at me and my NorCal slang than it was to critically analyze their hero.

The most alienated I ever felt in grad school was when I got my evaluation for "Intro to Clinical Skills." This was a course where you learned, among other things, how to "carry yourself" like a counselor. If you fidgeted with your hair, said "um" too much, or sat funny, they docked you points. You can guess what the instructor said about me. Actually, you don't have to guess; here is a direct quote from his evaluation:

> She has a tendency to get into a question-asking mode when an interpretation would be better to make. When anxious she stutters, which may be a limitation. However, having ability to acknowledge and talk [about] this situation is a big plus.

My stuttering is a manifestation of anxiety? Give me a break! Even Freud said, "Sometimes a cigar is only a cigar." In this case, and in most cases, a stutter is only a stutter. Some psychology professors become so full of themselves and their analytical powers, they think they can read a person's mind by counting the number of buttons on their shirt. Maybe instead of trying to read minds, you can just talk to people? The evaluation said I needed to make interpretations instead of asking questions; maybe he should have asked me a few questions before making interpretations about me!

The more exact I need to be with my language, the more I will stutter. And guess what? Graduate school is a place where you need to be exact with your language. Skating around difficult words by describing them isn't going to fly. I can say "Ventromedial Hypothalamus" and stutter, or I can say "that thingy in your brain that makes you less hungry" and not stutter. I'm not going to pretend like I'm ignorant just to appease someone's prejudice toward my speech.

I continued to encounter prejudice throughout my grad school experience. I had teachers questioning my accommodations. My learning disability and stuttering came under increasing scrutiny. I couldn't believe it. How could this kind of discrimination still be a thing? The Americans with Disabilities Act had been law for five years. It was the 90's, for fuck's sake! Did I fall through a wormhole and wind up back in 1980s Catholic school? It sure felt that way. Here I was, a capable and independent woman earning her degree, and one comment from an asshole professor could suddenly reduce me to a third grade girl all over again. I felt more and more hopeless, more and more isolated. So I started reaching out to other students with disabilities.

I never had friends with disabilities before, but I always felt a pull towards the Disability Community. Whenever I needed to write an essay on a famous person, I always chose Helen Keller. When I needed an elective in high school, I volunteered in the special education room. I loved working in that classroom, but I was also embarrassed to walk down the street with a group of students who had more apparent disabilities. Back then my goal was to conceal my differences; the last thing I wanted to do was outwardly identify with the part of me I was trying to hide. Sure, I had my experience with the NSP, but that was completely separate from my peer group. The idea of forming my social life around a disabled identity would have made my teenage self squirm.

But I wasn't in high school anymore. The fear of standing out seemed petty next to the reality of being marginalized. In my darkest moments, when it felt like I had no hope of ever succeeding in the academic world—when it felt like my entire future was a waste—I found strength in my disabled peers. Some of them had physical disabilities. Others had learning disabilities, like me. Someone even had a professor tell them, "If you still have a learning disability by the time you're in grad school, maybe you shouldn't be here." Suddenly I didn't feel so isolated. I wasn't the only one getting shitty treatment! I started to think about the problem in more political terms. Yes, we inherited victories like the ADA from the disability rights movement, but we also inherited a responsibility to keep that movement going. I became more outspoken and joined with other students to advocate for disability rights. At one point we even travelled to Washington DC for a rally on Capitol Hill.

Four and a half years and approximately ten billion dollars later, I finally graduated with my PsyD (doctorate in psychology). After all that hard work and sacrifice, the academic gods had accepted me into their good graces.

Just kidding! The hoop-jumping never ends. I was able to get some work as a disability advocate and adjunct professor, but nothing with upward mobility. I wasn't getting any speaking or full-time faculty positions, even though I was (and still am) a badass teacher. In graduate programs, there is a pressure to publish or perish. What you write is more important than any positive teacher evaluations; more important than any activism—unless that activism is submitted in writing, peer-reviewed, and published in a quarterly journal. That wasn't me. I could pull it off to some extent, but it was like writing in a second or third language. When it came to publish or perish, I definitely fell under the second category. No one wanted me to keynote or present. I had no selling points. I was dead in the water.

I spent many years looking for work in community colleges.

Community colleges are less focused on what you publish and more concerned about what you contribute to the campus. Incidentally, community college was the one place in my academic career where I felt at home. Teachers encouraged me. Accommodations were streamlined and easy to access. There were even counselors and other staff who had disabilities themselves. Out of the eight years I spent in college, my closest mentor was Dr. Jerry Egusa, the Learning Disability Specialist at Chabot College. He helped me navigate the teaching profession, which eventually led to me working as a counselor—and then a professor—at another community college. And I'm still there today. Comedians aren't supposed to talk about their "day jobs," but I've already told you everything else, so whatever. Now you know everything. Everything except how old I was when I lost my virginity. . . I'm going to the grave with that one.

I love stand-up comedy, but I also love having a steady job with a pension, benefits, and tenure. More importantly, I love working with my students. Many of them are the first in their family to go to college, like me. Many of them have disabilities, also like me. Many of them are discovering their academic potential and talents, despite what others said they could or could not acheive. Doing what I can to help them enjoy a fair and comfortable college experience is the ultimate payoff for all the bullshit I had to put up with in academia. The only drawback is not being able to drop as many F-bombs as I'd like, but that's what stand-up is for, right?

# 8
# Finding Utopia

In the summer of 2006, I saw something online about a Queer Disability Conference at San Francisco State University. Tickets were cheap, and the subject was relevant to my interests, so I decided to jump on it.

I imagined the entire Disability Community would be there. As it turned out, I was one of the few straight people in attendance. Even though I am not LGBT, the event held a lot of personal significance for me. I'll never forget when one of the keynote speakers, a woman using a wheelchair, proudly declared, "I could have fought for equality by going to grad school, but I'm going to make porn to fight the system instead!" After years of mothballing myself in the stuffy closet of academia, this was like a breath of fresh air.

I walked around the conference, taking in the scope of it. There were pamphlets and presentations and people representing all kinds of ideas. I made sure to watch the presentation on non-apparent disabilities. One of the panelists was Nora O'Connor from Passing Twice, an organization for queer people who stutter. When the presentation was finished, I walked over to Nora and introduced myself. We immediately hit it off.

I kept in touch with Nora after the conference. With her

encouragement, I slowly made my way back into the stuttering community. I went to events and got caught up on the scene. The NSP was still around but going by a different name, the National Stuttering Association (NSA). I started making connections and inroads. I even spoke on a panel for FRIENDS (an organization for kids who stutter, not the 90s sitcom about people who live in an apartment they could never afford in real life).

While these things gave me a sense of community and accomplishment, my overall life was still a mess. My academic career was going nowhere. I had written and published some articles, but nothing that advanced my status; I was working harder, not smarter, on the academic treadmill. I was still an adjunct professor teaching six classes a week, while simultaneously working as a full-time counselor for graduate students with disabilities. I taught more than any professor I knew, for zero recognition and pennies on the dollar.

If my professional life was stuck in a rut, my love life was drowning in a pit of quicksand. My relationships still had an average shelf-life of six months. Any guys who stuck around after that usually came with a mess of codependency issues. It got to the point where I was putting my boyfriend's needs above my own wellbeing. Ask not what he can do for you, but what you can do for him, etc.

While all this was going on, I came down with a nasty case of depression. My depression was a fickle and elusive creature, as it would only strike under certain conditions. Namely on weekends, or holiday breaks—whenever I had downtime, basically. I hated downtime. If I had a gap in my schedule, the depression would slip right in and make itself at home. I would crawl into bed, curl into the fetal position, and watch *Chappelle Show* re-runs until something required me to leave the house. Many times—most of the time—I couldn't name a specific reason for feeling sad. It just... happened. At least when I wasn't busy. As soon as I had something to work on and distract me from my thoughts, the depression would retreat back into its hole.

I decided to give my affliction a name: "Special ed depression."

I'm not saying that special ed causes depression. Far from it! Special education was the most nurturing and supportive learning environment I ever had. Aside from my parents and Elaine, my special ed teachers were the first adults to tell me that I had potential. I'll never forget one of my teachers, Ms. Bramlette. At my last IEP (Individualized Education Plan) meeting, Ms. Bramlette shared her thoughts from observing me at the preschool where I worked. She saw that I could rein in the attention of three-year-olds like no one else!

"Nina," she told me, "watching you do circle time was like watching Lily Tomlin. You were great!"

In one fell swoop, Ms. Bramlette had validated my teaching skills and my love for comedy. She had no idea that I wanted to be a comedian, or that I had a sock puppet of Edith Ann at home. So yeah, special ed was great!

The reason I call my condition special ed depression is because it came from internalizing the stigma placed on special ed students. I didn't see myself through Ms. Bramlette's eyes—not when I was feeling bad, anyway. I saw myself through the eyes of my Catholic school teachers who told my parents that I had no future. I saw myself through the eyes of bullies who make N-N-N-Nina jokes. I saw myself through the eyes of my instructors in grad school who heavily implied that I had no business being there. For all the people who supported and believed in me, these haters were still dictating my self-esteem.

I let myself be ruled by the voices of negativity. It's why I committed myself to unhappy relationships. It's why I felt sick whenever I stopped working and had time to be alone with my own brain. Because if I allowed myself to listen, I could hear it say, "You were in special ed and you don't deserve to be happy."

So that's why I call it special ed depression.

I knew I had to make a change, but I didn't know where to start. I continued doing what I was already doing. I worked with the disability community and went to events, occasionally securing gigs as a speaker. I worked my job as a college counsellor to students with disabilities, trying to guide them toward something better than my own college experience.

Then, in 2009, I got an idea. The school where I worked had a policy of sending me to an academic conference once a year. I could convince them to send me to the National Stuttering Association conference in Arizona! It turned out to be an easy sales pitch, since the NSA charges way less than your typical academic conference, and my employer liked to save a buck wherever they could. Whoever stamped the final invoice had no idea I was going for mainly personal reasons.

I had taken part in similar conferences before. As you'll recall, I even volunteered at an NSA conference in the summer after high school, back when they were still known as the NSP. But my involvement had always been strictly professional. It's the difference between going to Disneyland on vacation and going to Disneyland to work the pretzel booth. This conference was going to be my Disneyland vacation! Although there was more than enough intellectual value to make it work-related, these events are hardly limited to academics. As my friend Steve Danner says about the Little People of America conference, "We'd be swinging from the chandeliers if we could reach them!" For many people with disabilities, a conference is one of the few places where we get to let our hair down and just be ourselves. Now, imagine thousands of people, releasing all those pent-up feelings at once. So yeah, things can get a little wild. That natural high had me going for the entire conference, and all I drank was one skinny white Russian (a white Russian with skim milk... feel free to buy me one at the next conference).

There were many revelations at that conference, but what really struck me was seeing all the young women. Hearing them speak with such ease and confidence, it made me realize how much I had been holding my own voice back. A voice is more than just the sounds in your throat. It is how you express your needs, your dreams… everything that defines you! Your voice can convey your most authentic self, or it can be suppressed and twisted into something artificial. As far as I had come from the days of "weird Nina" in high school, I was still not being true to myself. I still refrained from speaking because I didn't want to inflict my stuttering on other people. It felt like I was trying to protect them, from the awkwardness of waiting through my blocks and repetitions. Or maybe I was really protecting myself, from the eye-rolls and looks of pity. If that meant not speaking up or offering my opinion, that was what I did.

People who stutter can easily sabotage themselves with avoidant behaviors. Like not introducing yourself because you're afraid of stuttering on your name. Or damaging a close friendship because you don't want to speak as the maid of honor at your friend's wedding. We resign ourselves to a lesser version of life, out of fear and social pressure. I find this problem especially compounded in women, since we're already taught to defer and yield to others. The next time you ride on public transit, see how many men have their legs spread in a "come and get it" stance, compared to the number of women with their legs crossed. We aren't supposed to take up too much space. It's as much an explicit order as it is a lifetime of social cues, beginning with childhood. When I was eleven years old, I was the reigning champ of *Mr. Do!* at the local arcade. No one could grab as many apples and cherries as I could. Then, one day when I was kicking ass and racking up a new high score, my grandmother Marie stood behind me and said, "Hurry up, other people are waiting to play!" I was taking up too much space. God forbid I should make someone else wait for their chance to override my initials on the leaderboard. Over time I took in more and more of these little cues, learning to minimize myself for the supposed sake of others.

By the time I got to that conference in 2008, I was several years deep into a lousy relationship with my boyfriend-at-the-time, Sean. And when I say "lousy," I mean it really (really) sucked. Our whole dynamic revolved around my low self-esteem and special ed depression. I hid entire parts of myself in order to make him more comfortable. Sure, I was open about my stutter, but I still made an effort to minimize it around him. I was a codependent caretaker trying not to take up too much space. There wasn't enough room for the full version of me.

Once, when I was invited on a radio show to discuss learning disabilities, I asked him not to listen, because I knew his comments would be unsupportive. As a disability advocate/expert, I needed to be as eloquent as possible, which meant I couldn't restrict my vocabulary to stutter-friendly words. Referring to the Americans with Disabilities Act as "that federal law the first George Bush passed" wasn't going to cut it. So I disclosed my stutter early in the interview and let my dysfluencies flow. When all was said and done, my boyfriend (who listened even though I asked him not to) had this to offer: "You stuttered a lot. It sounded like you were trying to stutter to be more down as a Disability advocate." Seriously? How much was I repressing myself around this guy, if he thought my natural voice sounded fake?

I spent the last night of the conference at a party in a hotel room. As I sat there watching the people around me, I was suddenly struck with an epiphany. Everyone was drinking, talking, laughing. Not a care in the world. I would never want to see them trapped in the type of cage I had built for myself. So why the hell should I live in it? The double standard was so ridiculous, I should have noticed it sooner. I was going to events and radio shows to advocate for equal treatment of people with disabilities, all while treating myself like garbage because of my disabilities. How messed up is that?

Change starts at home, and I needed to clean house. Even though I had made peace with stuttering in my professional life, I was still holding back in my personal life. That's just how it goes. People don't necessarily accept their disability all at once; many times we have to re-accept and re-embrace it in different parts of our life.

I spent the flight home thinking about what I wanted from my life. The answers had all been revealed in that conference. The way I minimized myself. The way I was afraid of stating my needs and taking up space. The way these things manifested in my current relationship. By the time I landed in Oakland, I knew that things were going to be different.

Five months later, I broke up with Sean. A couple of months after that, I started stand-up comedy. The root of my special ed depression had been yanked out. I was finally free to share my voice.

# 9
# The Brainwash Years (A Lot of Love)

The sitcom *Mama's Family* taught me how important the church can be to a community. In addition to serving as a place of worship, it provides a space for women's groups, pancake breakfasts, white elephant sales, and so much more. It seemed like Mama was always talking about something happening in her church, whether it was someone kissing up to the minister or deciding who has the best ambrosia to serve at the ladies' luncheon.

My Catholic upbringing wasn't exactly on par with the Mama Harper experience. My dad coached the Catholic Youth Organization girls' softball team, and my parents volunteered for pasta feeds and Bingo nights, but that was pretty much it. Our family would hop from church to church, always in search of the shortest Sunday mass with the least amount of singing. Our motto was "Get the communion and get out!" It was the spiritual equivalent of having your parking validated.

One thing I learned in church is that people have different reasons for being there. Some people come for what they need and leave (like my family waiting for communion and a post-wafer prayer before jetting out). Others get a little too involved (seriously, it's not the end of the world if the napkin colors don't match at the seniors' conference). Others are just there to schmooze. I remember a man at our church who was a local politician. Sometimes, after five o'clock mass, he would approach my family and say hello. My mom observed that he only did this when there was an election coming up.

That politician understood the power of the church as a networking tool. Religious communities offer connections that can lead to jobs, friendships, marriages, and more. Oh yeah, and there's also the spiritual part! Let's not forget about that. Religion can be personally transformative. For many people, the rituals of worship have a cleansing and grounding effect. When they are faced with crisis, religion offers them a formula for coping. Someone died? There are funeral rites. Feeling guilty about something you did? There are atonement rituals.

My relationship with the church never ran that deep. Once my parents stopped bringing me along, I was pretty much out, apart from a few obligatory family functions. I never had the experience of being an integral part of a church community. Not until I became a comedian and discovered the Brainwash.

Comparing the Brainwash Café and Laundromat[1] open mic to a church might sound like a bit of a leap, but it's a short leap. Both serve as communal spaces. Actually, the Brainwash served as three communal spaces: laundromat, café, and open mic. The holy trinity! You had washing machines in one room and a café/performance space in the other. You could get a beer and watch stand-up while waiting for your clothes to dry. A genius business model if there ever was one. Throughout the day, the drifters/yuppies/techies/druggies/hippies/rockers/skaters would come to eat, read, work on their laptops, hog the single-stall bathrooms, loiter, drink the free water, and do a million other things I probably don't want to know about. In a city increasingly shaped by economic barriers, the Brainwash offered the rarest example of a complete cross-section. You could sit at a table with techies pitching start-ups to your left and skater bros scoring drugs to your right. Around three o'clock, the early-bird comedians would start rolling in. You could tell them apart from the ordinary patrons (civilians) if you knew what clues to look for. They carried notebooks. They rarely bought anything. They always crowded around the same two tables outside, passing around a joint and running jokes by each other. Between five and six, they would start lining up at the back door to get a good spot on the sign-up sheet.

The Brainwash had a mic going two or three nights a week, but Thursday was the big one—the Sunday service, if you will. Thursday nights were hosted by Tony Sparks, AKA the Godfather of San Francisco Comedy. He was the pastor of this degenerate church, leading the crowd through another evening mass. I had seen Tony on a show in Oakland fifteen years before I ever called myself a comedian, so I knew his legend long before I signed up for my first set at the Brainwash.

If it was your first time signing up, Tony would tell you to put a star next to your name. When it was your turn to perform, Tony would scream at the top of his lungs:

TONY:
Hey good humans! Your next comedian is new to the room,
so what do we give them?!

AUDIENCE:
A lot of love!

TONY:
Say it louder!

AUDIENCE:
A LOT OF LOVE!!!

TONY:
That's right! Everyone, I want you to lose your fucking minds for [insert frightened newcomer's name here]!!!

On that cue, the gathered assortment of comedians, Google worker bees, and confused laundry patrons would erupt into applause—the loudest your average open mic performer would probably ever hear. The crowd's enthusiasm would then gently diminish as they watched the first-time performer fumble through their badly-written material and realize that wow, this is actually hard! After five underwhelming minutes, Tony would get back on stage and act like he had just seen the greatest talent in the history of stand-up (then forget about them two seconds later and bring up the next act). Just like that, another congregant had been baptized into the church of SF comedy by Tony Sparks.

If Tony was the minister of the Brainwash, the deacons were people like Anthony Medina and Kristee Ono. When it wasn't Thursday, they held open mics and showcases that gave us great sets, painful lessons, and everything in between. Kristee even organized a comedy prom night—perhaps the only time I'll ever get to do stand-up in a formal with my grandmother Ida's mink stole. I was definitely not too weird for that prom!

Just like church, the Brainwash had its own set of rituals and practices, which went something like this:

- Don't run the light

- Bring your own pen when you sign up

- Women sign up first

- If you are not a woman, get there early

- Don't run the light
- Expect a contact buzz when entering on the café side
- Don't come in late and expect Tony to put you up, unless you've been on TV
- Expect comedians who have been on TV to show up late and jump ahead of you on the list
- Watch out for Sweet Gail, she might hit you with her cane
- If you're running the light, get the fuck off stage!

These were the customs we all observed. No matter how important you thought you were. No matter what was going on in your life. No matter your education or status. None of that mattered at the Brainwash. All that mattered was being funny and not running the light. There were rare exceptions, like the night when Faizon Love (Big Worm in *Friday*) came through. The drunk hipsters were so star-struck, he could have committed a war crime on stage and they would have eaten it up. I can still hear the voice of the guy sitting behind me, gushing to his friend, "Oh my God! It's Faizon! FAIZON!" I saw firsthand how a big fish can show up to a small pond and get all the adoration they want for doing next to nothing. The rest of us had to win the crowd over by being funny. And sometimes even that wasn't enough.

Just like church, the Brainwash provided a space to network and socialize. You could form friendships, romantic or sexual relationships (which Tony strongly advised against), and get booked for other shows. My first paid gig was the result of Tony introducing me to Kiko Breiz, who produced a show called Speech Therapy (how fitting is that?). The Brainwash also introduced me to Jabari Davis, who booked me on a show at the historic Purple Onion club. Because of the Brainwash, I got to perform on a stage where legends like Lenny Bruce, The Smothers Brothers, and Phyllis Diller once stood.

The majority of my comedian friends are people I met at the Brainwash: my friend (and current neighbor) Heather, who first caught my attention with her bit about feeling guilty for going on a luxury cruise; my friend O.J., who documented the San Francisco comedy scene on his blog, Courting Comedy; my friend Jesse, who impressed everyone with his unusual brain; and, of course, Mean Dave! I remember the moment when Dave and I became real friends. We were laughing at this one comic for blatantly kissing the host's ass, bonding over our shared distaste for ass-kissing in general. At some point the conversation turned to Dave's sick grandmother, a nice British lady in a convalescent home. I told him about the experience I had with my own grandma passing. That was when I knew Dave was a real friend and not just a peer in stand-up.

The Brainwash was a place where you discovered friends. It was also a place where you discovered who wasn't your friend. Unlike church, stand-up allows people with beef to openly rip on each other, on and off the stage. Sometimes a little teasing would dispel the tension. Other times it poured gas on the fire. I once had a comedian make fun of my stuttering and say, "It's okay because my uncle stutters." He was Asian American, so I said, "I have Filipino cousins; that doesn't mean I get to make hacky jokes about Asian people." When I got up on stage that night, I spent four minutes mocking his fluent entitlement while he ducked out the side door. I guess it got too hot for him to handle.

As I became more comfortable and established at the Brainwash, I no longer felt compelled to explain my stuttering at the beginning of every set. People knew who I was; I could jump right into my observations about something unrelated to disability and not worry about them fixating on my speech. I came to realize that open mics are for the comedians and not the audience. It's our time to experiment, workshop ideas, and socialize. Sometimes we only have three minutes to try out all our new material—you think I'm going to waste two of those minutes on a generic disclaimer? It eventually got to the point where new comedians would come up to me and ask, "Have you ever thought about mentioning stuttering in your act?" Nope . . . never thought of that. Thanks for the tip!

As if it weren't already perfect, the Brainwash had four pinball machines in the laundry area. My two favorite things in life are comedy and pinball! Did I mention that I'm a world ranked player? If you ever look at a pinball machine and see "NAG" on the leaderboard, you'll know who was there! Someone once told me that I'm probably in the top two percent of female players. That same person also offered me a foot rub, but I choose to believe he wasn't just making up those statistics to hit on me.

One night I was there playing Junkyard, one of my all-time favorite machines (that's the one where you have to assemble a junk-mobile to defeat Crazy Bob in space . . . as one does). I could hear Tony Sparks in the other room, leading the audience in another baptism: "What do we give them? A LOT OF LOVE!"

I listened in on the newbie's set. He had one-liners that were smart and funny, especially for his first time on stage. Something jingle-jangled and pulled my attention back to the pinball table. Gotta watch out for that swinging crane!

I was still concentrating on the game when I saw Tony from the corner of my eye. He was introducing that new kid to an older, more experienced comedian. The latter was about my age, doing the unbuttoned-dress-shirt-over-a-T-shirt look with an army messenger bag on the side.

"Here, talk to him," said Tony. He was clearly pawning this energetic rookie onto another comic so he could get back to hosting and finishing his burger and fries.

As I collected more junk to build my spacecraft and kill Crazy Bob, I eavesdropped on their conversation. The young neophyte was asking questions nonstop, picking the brain of this veteran comic. I was less than a year in myself, and no seasoned comic would ever give me the time of day. They tend to be the like blue-haired rich ladies in church, unable to bother with anyone beneath them in the Constituency. This guy wasn't like that. He listened to the new kid and patiently answered all of his questions, though he must have been secretly annoyed at Tony for sticking him with babysitting duty. I willfully lost to Crazy Bob so I could join the conversation. I told the new kid that his style reminded me of Emo Philips, which made him all giddy because apparently he worshipped Emo. After another fifteen minutes of conversation, the new kid ran off to do some more networking. It was just me and the other guy now. We introduced ourselves; he said his name was Ethan.

"You were really patient and nice to the new comic," I said. "Were you ever a special ed teacher or something like that?"

It turned out that Ethan was in fact a teacher, and he had worked in a program for adults with disabilities. When you grow up in special ed, you develop a sixth sense for these things.

Ethan and I had a lot in common. We were both on the introverted side. We both had a habit of offering rides to other comics. We eventually formed a carpool together, along with two other comedians. As I felt myself becoming more attracted to Ethan, I started to scrutinize him in greater detail. Tony strongly advises against dating other comics, and I was very hesitant at the idea. If Ethan and I were going to date, he had to pass two tests. First, he couldn't be a scumbag: no rape jokes, no womanizing. Second, he had to be funny. I remember watching him perform and thinking, "Okay, this is it. If he doesn't make me laugh, I can't have a crush on him anymore." I am happy to say that he passed both of my tests!

One day Ethan asked me out to lunch. We went to an Indian restaurant, followed by a trip to Yogurt Park in Berkeley. Ethan got zazzleberry-flavored yogurt topped with Oreos and gummy worms—does the thought of that make you also want to throw up?

We spent the rest of the day strolling around and talking, until he had to leave for a show in San Francisco. He texted me later that night: "Is it a disability to have a crush on someone?" I texted back, "Only if it impairs your daily life functions." He confirmed that it did. We went on several more dates, and things started to get serious.

On November 5th, 2016, Ethan and I were married at the Madonna Inn.[2] My bridesmaids were my closest friends: Gina, Heather, Jody, and Mean Dave. Even though they are all talented writers, they elected Dave to give the bridesmaid speech.

"I hate weddings," he began, raising his glass to toast. "If you told me when I started stand-up comedy at the Brainwash that in six years I'd be a bridesmaid in a wedding, saying the wedding toast to two aspiring comedians from that very same open mic... I would have quit comedy right then and there."

The Brainwash wove our lives together in ways none of us could have predicted.

You might have noticed that I keep referring to the Brainwash in the past tense. Sadly, it was forced to shut down in December, 2017—another casualty of the changing culture and economics of San Francisco. The end came suddenly and without warning. One day some comedians showed up for the open mic and found locked doors instead. There was a letter from the owner taped to the window, listing the reasons that are always listed when another San Francisco landmark vanishes overnight. Bay Area comedians collectively lost their shit. Their brain pathways were wired to go to the Brainwash on Thursdays! Like Skinner rats pushing the disconnected food button, they sulked in front of the empty building out of pure habit and faith. Others ranted and raged through social media, which is kind of ironic, seeing how the Brainwash was killed by dot-com-fueled development. The rest of us grieved quietly.

The Brainwash was our church. It was our community and home.

The building might be demolished or converted into an upscale condo, but the things that happened there can never unhappen. Memories were made and lives were changed. Countless friendships exist because of the Brainwash. The careers of famous and unfamous comedians exist because of the Brainwash. This book, the one you're reading right now, exists because of the Brainwash.

Not bad for an open mic in a laundromat.

# 10
# D-D-Dating's Weird...

Hurl a stone through an open mic and it will probably whack a comedian in the head as they exclaim, "Dating's weird, am I right?" That one phrase has become so cliché that it is cliché to point out that it is cliché. It's cliché squared. But that doesn't change the simple fact that *dating is weird*. And it's even weirder when you stutter.

When I broke up with Sean, online dating was a firmly established "thing." Everyone who wasn't married had tried it at least once. Everyone except me, of course. The last time I had been single, people were using dial-up modems. The entire game had changed and I didn't know where to start. Dating is already bad enough, but now I had to do it through profiles and private messages like some kind of e-Bay auction? Gross!

I recruited one of my guy friends to help me fill out the questions on my OkCupid profile. He was an old pro at this online dating thing, so I knew I could count on him for good suggestions.

**The first thing people usually notice about me...**
*"My eyes are UP HERE BOYS"*

Okay, maybe not. At least his intentions were good.

My profile ended up being mostly references to comedy and pinball. Under "**I spend a lot of time thinking about…**" I wrote, "How to make bunk beds so I have more room to do activities!" You might recognize that line from *Stepbrothers*, the Will Ferrell movie about two grown men who act like five-year-olds and share a room in their parents' house. That's romantic, right?

Actually, the comedy stuff landed me a few dates. Most of them were hooked by my various allusions to Chris Elliot. Forget the wonky algorithms; any man who loves *Cabin Boy* has to be a good match, right? Once a guy was interested, the next step was communicating with him via private message. If we exchanged decent banter, I would initiate the next step and set up a date.

It turns out that a man can love *Cabin Boy* and still be boring. Who knew? Every date was the same awkward conversation over the same overpriced hipster fried chicken with the same splitting of the check. There was no second date. Good! My new life as a comedian had given me an allergy to unfunny men. Most dates had me counting the minutes until I could say goodbye and escape to an open mic.

But I couldn't get off the OkCupid train that easy. I had to keep trying! Keep tooling and retooling my profile until it attracted the right kind of man! I spent an inordinate amount of time on my profile, agonizing over how to present myself and how others would read it. The hardest part, of course, was figuring out how to mention the stuttering elephant in the room.

## You should really contact me if…
*"You have a stuttering fetish"*

Funny, but it might attract the wrong kind of attention.

# I am good at...
*"Making fun of people who make fun of my stuttering."*

That's better. A warning shot to scare away the jerks.

I went through many more revisions, searching in vain for that perfect way to broach the subject of my speech. How you disclose a disability is serious stuff. It can make or break a first impression. And in our ridiculous society, a handful of first impressions can determine a person's whole future.

When people ask me if they should mention their disability on a job application, I always respond with a cautious "no." Better safe than sorry—and I have been sorry before. When I was applying for internships during my final year of grad school, I had the option to apply to ten different agencies, many of them colleges. I mentioned my stuttering and learning disabilities in the cover letter, explaining how my personal experience could be helpful in mentoring students with similar backgrounds. I don't think my prospective employers agreed. From those ten applications, I got two invitations for an interview. That was the first and last time I decided to disclose my disabilities in a cover letter.

I have made a policy of not disclosing my stuttering until the actual interview. I mean, at that point my stuttering is going to disclose itself whether I like it or not. So I walk in there and own it. I tell the interviewer, "I stutter and you are just going to have to wait for all the brilliant things I have to say." I find that my playful but confident tone removes any ambiguity and puts the room at ease. I don't say anything about my learning disability until I get the job.

Some people think I'm dishonest for not coming clean with all my disabilities up front. Because everyone else treats job interviews like their deathbed confession, right? So what if an employer unknowingly hires someone with dyslexia to do a job that isn't impaired by dyslexia? I can only imagine how hard it must be, to have a qualified

employee who fulfills the responsibilities of their job but spells something wrong when they sign a birthday card in the breakroom…

So what does all this have to do with dating? Everything!

I've always said that dating is like the job market. Whether it's an
interview or a first date, the process is basically the same: you smile,
do the song-and-dance routine, and then go home to wait by your
phone for a week. During this courtship period you have to play your
cards close to the chest and put on a happy poker face. The real you
doesn't get to come out until you've passed the final callback, whenever your prospective employer/partner decides that is.

My adventure in online dating had become an unsolvable puzzle
of self-censorship. Which parts of me was I supposed to show? How
much do I save for the first date? The second? The third? Marriage? I
had to think long and hard about which cards to play and which ones
to hold. I began to realize that maybe OkCupid wasn't the place to
talk about disability. Guys would read my profile and assume the part
about stuttering was a joke. I don't blame them. People are mostly
familiar with stuttering in a joke context (e.g., Looney Toons), and
my tone was jokey to begin with. What's a single stuttering comedian
supposed to do?

I decided to up my game. Whenever I had plans to meet a guy,
I would send him a message along the lines of, "Hey, I just wanted
you to know that I stutter. Here is some more information if you are
interested." I would then link him to a webpage explaining the basics
of stuttering and good practices for etiquette.

The link approach got mixed results. Some guys ignored it.
Others read the whole thing and made a conscious effort. One guy,
an adjunct professor who was trying reeeeally hard, decided to take
it one step further and conduct additional research, which led him
to some of my writing. It might sound sweet, but it was also kinda
stalky (Sweet n' Stalky, America's favorite dipping sauce). I guess I
shouldn't be talking, since I looked him up on RateMyProfessor.com.

Many students described him as boring (after the date, I came to the conclusion that they might be onto something).

One guy responded to my link with outright dismissal. "It sounds like you're not ready to date yet," he wrote back. Well buddy, if everyone were as enlightened as you, maybe I wouldn't need to send the damn link! I'm not ready to date yet? Is OkCupid only reserved for those who have achieved perfect self-actualization and transcended the physical plane to become luminous beings of pure energy with zero hang-ups in life? We actually did go on a few dates after that. I ended up liking him more than most of the other guys.

After going through so many rounds of the online dating game, I decided to bring it up with my therapist, Dr. J.

Dr. J is the best therapist ever. He isn't the stereotypical shrink with click-clack balls on his desk, dissecting your brain behind a legal pad. He is warm and grounded, an African-American surfer dude in his sixties with seashell tattoos. I love watching him feed peanuts to the squirrels outside his window; they line up like cartoon animals on Snow White's balcony, snatching their dry-roasted treats from the fingers of this magical man. Oh yeah, did I mention that he's also awesome at his job? Dr. J has helped me through so many challenges, whether it's stuttering stuff or relationship stuff or family stuff or comedy stuff. He was there to talk me through my initial fears of becoming a performer and cheer me on into becoming the Nina I am today.

I told Dr. J about my troubles with online dating, and the challenge of presenting myself in the right light. I told him about disclosing my stuttering and sending guys a link before the first date. He stopped me right there.

"Why do you do that?" he asked.

"Because I'm supposed to be on a date. I don't want to waste the whole time educating them on stuttering. They aren't paying me!"

"Really, Nina?"

"Yes really! I'm not educating anyone unless they pay me or I'm performing on stage. They can learn this stuff on their own time!"

"You've taught me a lot about stuttering. And I didn't pay you."

He had me there.

Dr. J suggested that most people don't know about the nuances of stuttering because they haven't been exposed to people with that kind of experience. He told me that part of a relationship is sharing those experiences. As the relationship grows and progresses, there will be times when more sharing and explanation are needed, which is why communication channels need to remain open.

I was hesitant to accept this explanation. I mean, how could he really know where I was coming from? As if reading my thoughts, Dr. J offered an example from his own life, specifically as a black man married to a white woman. His relationship with his wife, in the larger context of American society, often required them to explain their experiences to each other. He told me how she once got frustrated because he couldn't keep up with her in a crowd. Dr. J had to explain to her that he didn't share her privilege in that space. She could be more aggressive and squeeze between a pack of strangers. If he did that, many people would perceive it as threatening. Dr. J and his wife were able to build a successful marriage because they were able to learn from each other in these situations.

Hearing this put my own situation into perspective. I realized that if you want to be in a relationship, you have to help the other person understand what it's like to be in your shoes. Letting them know your personal preferences, wishes, and experiences is all part of the deal. I couldn't just paste a URL link. I had to create a personal link through ongoing, mutual exchange.

A few months later, my days of online dating came to an end. Ethan and I had known each other for about six months, hanging out at open mics and carpooling to shows. As a fellow comedian, he knew my act and where I was coming from—as a performer and as a person. I didn't have to worry about sending links or writing profiles; my stand-up reflected my personality and life experience better than any website.

Oh yeah, and we watch *Stepbrothers* every time it's on TV. I guess it's a romantic movie after all?

# 11

# The Three-Hour Comedy Anxiety Attack

One of the most memorable sets I ever had was, of all places, in the back of an Italian restaurant in Fremont, California.

I was amped for this show! Me performing at an Italian restaurant? I figured I was good as family (insert hacky Olive Garden joke here). When I got there and saw the audience with their olive complexions and noses shaped like mine, my hopes were instantly confirmed. These were my people! I could stutter in front of these strangers and they would accept me as one of their own. Making random people giggle at dick jokes is one thing, but in this room we could share a cathartic laugh over the sort of cultural in-jokes and serious subjects that only families can talk about.

I could tell stories about things other audiences just wouldn't get. Like when someone in my family revealed to us that she was a lesbian. My grandmother dealt with the news by pretending not to know what a lesbian was. Yeah. This went on for twenty-five years! After a quarter-century of humoring this bullshit, I decided one day to finally spell it out: "She's a lesbian, Ma! She doesn't want to kiss men! She kisses women!" My grandmother's response was, "Oh, I didn't know that's what that meant all this time." Yuh, right! She might as well have claimed to be a virgin. A regular crowd might find this funny enough, but you need that extra layer of cultural context to fully appreciate the pathological streak of denial that runs in my family.

There were a million stories I could tell to this audience, but it's usually best to open with established material. I walked on stage and delivered my best jokes on stuttering, channeling my excitement into the performance.

I got crickets. Worse than crickets, because crickets don't actively hate you. These people gave me bitter humphs and looks of contempt. I moved on to dirtier jokes, which also bombed. The audience seemed to hate me even more for trying to win them back. Back from what? These assholes hated me from the start! I could practically hear their thoughts: "Why are you talking about this in public? We don't want your shame. Women aren't supposed to talk/sound like that. Bury your feelings and deal with them yourself."

I couldn't do that. Comedy is about addressing the truth. Instead of burying my feelings and feeding these people the cheap, Jeff Dunham-style jokes they clearly wanted, I was determined to break through their antipathy and find some common ground. Doing unrehearsed material for a hostile crowd is rarely a good idea, but at that point I had nothing to lose. I shifted gears and went into my personal stories about Italian family stuff. I joked about how Italian-Americans like to take unnecessary precautions based on urban legends, how we worry that space heaters and televisions will kill you because someone's uncle heard a "story" about someone else's uncle getting blown up or electrocuted. I talked about my grandmother and how she was afraid of me riding the Matterhorn at Disneyland, because she claimed that her cousin's cousin stood up on the roller-coaster and got decapitated (um. . . sure). The audience didn't budge an inch. Maybe they didn't appreciate hearing about blood and guts while trying to eat their spaghetti and meatballs. I don't care. They were jerks.

I got off stage early. Who cares if my fifteen minutes weren't up? That shit felt like fifteen hundred. The producer of the show ran a comedy competition that I had won earlier in the year, so at least he knew I was capable of making an audience laugh. I thanked him for having me and got the hell out of there.

I found my Jeep in the oversized strip mall parking lot and flopped into the driver's seat. Driving usually calms me down and helps me process my emotions. I didn't even make it out of the lot before I started crying. I don't mean some wimpy little sniffles; this was full-on snot-bubble toddler-who-needs-to-leave-the-store-type crying. By the time I got home, my sobbing fit had spiraled into a three-hour anxiety attack.

I told Ethan what happened. He tried to console me with stories of him bombing (very sweet of him), but I was inconsolable. The heavy crying continued. Back then I lived a block away from my parents in Oakland, so we walked over there to see if they could help.

As I told my mom and dad what happened, it became clear this wasn't about comedy. I've had crowds that don't get me. I've had crowds that do get me and hate me anyway. I've been heckled head to toe in bars and clubs and websites across America and some parts of Europe. I've bombed on every stage and makeshift structure pretending to be a stage you can imagine. I've had hipsters give me dirty hipster looks and yuppies give me dirty yuppie looks. I've performed for "disability awareness" college events only to have the students make fun of my stutter. But did I cry after any of those shows? Not once!

So why was this different?

This was about family.

In traditional Italian-American culture, women aren't supposed to be funny. Unless we are reading poems at a funeral or serving cake, we are expected to be fairly quiet. It's a real shame too, because we clearly have a talent for running our mouths (Joy Behar, Lisa Lampanelli and Janeane Garofalo come to mind).

Oh, and we are definitely NOT supposed to talk about shameful things like disabilities and family secrets (two of my favorite topics!). So where does that leave me? For the people in the back of that restaurant, the intersection of my culture, gender, and disability came together to form something unacceptable. The sum of my parts had canceled me out, like positive and negative numbers adding up to zero. I drove home from the show, feeling like my entire existence was going to unravel. The final gut-punch was the unconscious realization that this is how my own family sees me.

I'm not talking about my parents—you already know they're amazing. And to all the other family members reading this: I'm not talking about you either. The ones I'm talking about don't even know about this book, and if they did, they would probably put it down halfway through the table of contents.

I'm talking about the backward cranks still dangling on the upper branches of my extended family tree. Many of them are from my grandparents' generation, with one foot in the mainstream and one foot in the Old World. They come from a culture where women are the caregivers, where our purpose in life is making others comfortable. I'm all about hospitality, but there's no way I'm wearing that hat all the time! Stand-up comedy and disability issues aren't exactly known for making people comfortable!

My family has a way of ignoring things that make them uncomfortable. My grandmother pretending not to know what lesbians are, for instance. A lot of my relatives adopted a similar tactic with me, preferring to sweep my speech (and even my opinions) under the rug. One year at Christmas, my great uncle was going on a diatribe about Mexican-American immigrants and how they shouldn't be able to vote. "If you want to vote, you should learn English," he said. I was in college at the time, reaching the point when young people start to develop a sense of moral conviction. "Wait a minute," I said, "didn't your own father never learn English? Wouldn't it have been nice for him to know that he was actually voting for JFK?" My uncle didn't answer; the sexist fire in his eyes said everything. From that point on, I no longer existed to him. It was the last conversation we ever had. I realized that if I wanted to be accepted by my family, my opinions would have to be toned down or omitted altogether.

Bombing in the Italian restaurant brought all these memories and feelings back with a vengeance. Talking about it with my parents helped, but the pain was still there. I walked back home, cried myself to sleep, woke up, went to work, and got on with life. But I continued thinking about my place in Italian-American culture and the questions raised by that show.

I spent a lot of time thinking about when my grandmother passed away. I've always thought of Grandma Ida as representing the best parts of my heritage. She was kind and caring. She insisted on feeding anyone who set foot in her home, always ready with a plate of petrified biscotti that could probably stay crunchy in milk for two days. We came from different worlds, and many aspects of my life were like an alien language to her, but she always showed me unconditional love. When I got my doctorate, I chose to have the graduation party at St. Philip Neri's hall, because it was only a block from her house and she had a fear of going places. That was the day she told me I was her "favorite granddaughter." I mean, I was her only granddaughter by blood, but still. I was moved.

Five years later, she had a stroke. Knowing the end was near, I took time off from my job to visit her with my parents, Auntie Norma, and Uncle Fred. We spent every day and many nights in the convalescent home, sleeping in chairs at her bedside. On one of those nights, I woke up at 2:00 AM in a sudden, inexplicable panic. Everything seemed normal, so I went outside to take a breather. I came back ten minutes later and found the entire family plus two nurses surrounding my grandmother's deathbed. She took her last breath right as I walked into the room. I still wonder if her departing spirit caused the random panic that jolted me awake ten minutes earlier, to drive me out of the room so I wouldn't have to experience the trauma of watching her die. That's the kind of person she was.

And now that person was gone. When Grandma Ida died, it felt like my cultural heritage had died with her—a large part of it, anyway.

The traditional Italian-American funeral has very specific roles. Who sits in which row, who carries the coffin, who does the readings, who gets to speak—these are all strictly predetermined. As a granddaughter, the only thing I was allowed to do was read a scripture. As you can imagine, reading out loud in front of large groups isn't exactly my jam. I wasn't comfortable with the idea of regaling everyone with a passage from John 14:2, especially under these circumstances, so that was off the table. I couldn't carry the coffin; only the men were allowed to do that. So I would have no role in my favorite grandparent's funeral, because I was a dyslexic woman who stuttered.

You can imagine the thoughts that were racing through my head when I pulled into the parking lot at Saint Philip's. My parents' friends, Bob and Sydney, were the first to greet me. I opened my mouth to say something, and the emotions just came tumbling out. "I have a vagina which means I don't get to do anything!" I cried, probably louder than I should have in front of a church. Sydney glanced at Bob, who quietly whisked me off to the vestibule where my dad was.

My dad offered to have me stand next to him carrying the coffin. I decided against it, thinking I would look weird as the hanger-on of a coffin procession. We agreed that I would speak. No reading, no scripture. Just me, talking. I spoke for three minutes, sharing memories of Grandma Ida and what she meant to me. I invoked her little gestures, the way she would shrug her shoulders and splay her palms, as if to say, "Whatever you want is fine." She was always easy-going and accepting like that. I was able to honor her the way I wanted to, because my family made an exception to the rules of tradition. Our culture didn't always provide the flexibility I needed as a woman or person with a disability, but here it was modified so that I could participate on my own terms. I know if Grandma Ida were there, she would have just smiled and given a little shrug.

I recently met another Italian-American woman at a stuttering conference. During that conversation, we identified a common theme in our experiences: stuttering is not something you do openly, because it might make someone uncomfortable.

When a culture designates women as caregivers, those women are expected to make other people comfortable. Grandma Ida had her biscotti for anyone who stepped through the door. No one leaves my house without first browsing my collection of teas and granola bars. Providing hospitality is an important skill that strengthens families, friendships, and communities. But it turns into a problem when "making people comfortable" means removing entire parts of yourself. I would always go the extra mile to conceal my stutter at family functions. Relatives would come up to my parents and say, "My, Nina's speech has gotten so much better!" Little did they know I was faking it for their benefit. My most effective trick for stuttering less? Talking less. I was minimizing myself for their sake. That is what happens when the caregiver role gets pushed too far.

I don't want to oversimplify the gender roles of an entire culture, but sometimes it can fit like an Italian leather stiletto—good-looking, but restrictive. I thought about using movie references to relate a more nuanced picture, but then I realized there aren't any good examples of women in Italian American cinema. We tend to take a backseat to the DeNiros and Pacinos of the genre. Feminist critiques of the *Godfather* films often point out the passive roles of characters like Kate and Connie. Coppola attempted to correct this in *The Godfather Part III,* but the film was considered a flop. Funny how the movie that features women in a larger role is considered the worst of the trilogy!

Oddly enough, the best depiction of women in an Italian American family comes from *My Big Fat Greek Wedding*. Just substitute "Italian" for "Greek" and "there you go." Like Nia Vardalos' character, we are pressured to devote ourselves as mothers, wives, grandmothers—roles defined by our place in the reproductive cycle. Whenever my cousins came to visit from Italy, the only questions they would ask me were, "Do you have a boyfriend?" and, "Why not?" When I told them I was in school and didn't have time for boys, they had no idea what to say. "The Italian word for college is *università*," one of them offered. Thanks, cousin Enrico. It was nice that he was trying to connect, but it was only after running out of ways to define me in relation to men.

I like to think that I learned something from my three-hour comedy anxiety attack. Some issues run deep, and when I encounter certain situations, old wounds will reopen. The good news is that the wounds hurt less after you acknowledge and talk about them. If I ever bomb in the back of another Italian restaurant, hopefully I won't have another three-hour anxiety attack. Maybe it will be two hours. The pain is still there, and that's okay. Because I was forced to confront those feelings, I can now process them more efficiently. I won't know how efficiently until my next existential crisis, but at least then I'll have a point of reference. If nothing else, the incident served as a reminder that I need to lead my own life. I don't have time to get caught up in the dysfunctional shame and restrictive gender roles that ruled over previous generations in my family. I have to be true to myself and just imagine my grandmother, smiling and shrugging with approval.

I'd like to end things on a lighter note, so in the spirit of comedy and Grandma Ida, I'll tell you her favorite joke (apologies in advance for the implied derogatory language):

"What is there to do in Italy?"

"Watch the day go!"

Get it? No? I guess old-fashioned words like "dago" (an offensive term for an Italian person) have rightfully fallen out of use. But if you came through Ellis island as a kid in 1916, it would have been hilarious! Well, maybe . . .

# 12
# Nina's Chappelle Show

I was unfashionably early for the open mic at Oakland's New Parish. After waiting outside for an eternity, maybe twenty minutes, the doors finally opened. A staff member quietly stepped out and propped up a sandwich board on the sidewalk. The words read, "Open Mic! Dave Chappelle hosting."

Dave Chappelle?!! I could barely contain myself. The chance to meet one of your comedy idols is exciting enough, but to perform on a show with them? Sure, I just happened to be standing outside the right door at the right time, but I still get bragging rights. Let me hip you to a little comedy secret: those of us who don't get consistent club work often fall ass-backwards into our credits. In other words, when I put "Performed with [big name comic]" on my resume, what I really mean is "[big name comic] made a surprise appearance on [small local show] where I happened to be performing." They don't hire me to open for them, and they rarely ever watch my set. Does that stop me from saying I've worked with them? Hell no! Especially if we're talking about a legend like Dave Chappelle.

I have always admired comedians who deliver social commentary from a unique perspective. Dave Chappelle is the perfect example. At the height of its popularity, *The Chappelle Show* confronted topics that everyone else was afraid to touch. Sketches like "When Keeping It Real Goes Wrong – Vernon Franklin" and "Frontline – Clayton Bigsby" provide hilarious commentary without sugarcoating for mainstream white audiences.[1] When I started doing stand-up, I looked to these sketches as a guide for how to joke about Disability without selling out.

And now here I was, about to sign up for an open mic hosted by Dave Chappelle. If it weren't for the sandwich board out front, you'd have never guessed there was something big going down in the New Parish. It looked like your ordinary Tuesday mic, i.e., way too many comics and no real audience. I sat at the bar and started mulling over my notebook. I had to make this performance count. I was so caught up in preparing for my set that I barely remember Chappelle walking out on stage.

At some point I took out my phone and relayed the situation to my parents. For whatever reason, my mom feels the need to bear witness to any spectacle happening within a fifteen-mile radius. It's why she saw Barry Bonds hit his 755th home run, even though she doesn't care about baseball. It's why she dragged us across the Bay Bridge to see a water stain shaped like the Virgin Mary. So you better believe that she and my dad were front and center to see me perform with the most famous comedian we cared about.

This wasn't my first time seeing Dave Chappelle live. I had seen him perform three times in the previous year alone! Two of those performances were at the New Parish, where I watched him do four consecutive hours of stand-up (I never got bored for a second). The third time was at a Black Star concert, where he gave a much shorter performance. It seemed like a bad environment for comedy, with everyone standing around drunk and waiting for the music to start, but I was excited to be there. I was fresh from breaking up with Sean and ready to enjoy life as a free woman. When Chappelle said, "Hip-hop shows are always a sausage fest," I gave an enthusiastic "Wooooo!" from the front row.

That got his attention. He glanced my way and added, "There's always a fat white girl at a rap show trying to pick up on guys." Keep in mind I was twenty pounds lighter than I am now. The comment stung until I remembered who said it. Did Dave Chappelle, one of my idols, really just make fun of me?! I swooned. I was so happy to be roasted by a great comedian, even if it was a hacky line on his part.

Remembering these experiences, I sat and planned for my set at the New Parish. Dave had been making fun of the other comedians all night, so it was a safe bet that he would notice my stutter and comment on it. My only hope was to get him before he got me, but in a way that also paid homage to one of my idols—a tricky task for any comedian, especially in her first year of stand-up!

When Chappelle introduced me, I gave him a hug. That's what you do when you meet someone famous, right? He handed me the microphone and I immediately proceeded with my best stuttering jokes. It was going well. Towards the end of my set, I told the story of how Dave Chappelle called me fat at the Black Star show. "I never thought that I would have the opportunity to address the comment, but since I am here, I have something to say . . ." I paused for effect. "Dave, you have always been an inspiration to me and you taught me how to blend social justice and comedy, and so it is with great honor that I say FUCK YOU DAVE! I was a fat child and that shit hurt! Go fuck yourself!" The audience cheered. We all love Dave Chappelle, but the power differential made me the underdog in this fight. I handed the microphone back to him and we hugged a second time (because again, famous person). As I got off stage and headed back to my seat, I knew I was in for it.

Chappelle quickly responded, "I might have said that, and I would like to apologize for calling you fat because I didn't know you stutter." Again, I swooned! Dave was making fun of me, only this time I had set the stage for it. It was on my terms. He went on to joke that I was now sexy/not fat and that he could "help with [my] stutter." Then, after a pause (I suspect he was censoring himself), he said that watching my set was like watching the first five minutes of Spike Lee's *Do The Right Thing.*[2] He then did an imitation of Smiley: "M-M-M-Mookie… M-M-M-Malcolm…" For those who haven't seen the movie, Smiley was a symbolic Greek tragedy-type character who stuttered (possibly due to cerebral palsy) and sold postcards of civil rights leaders.

Chappelle changed the subject and did another thirty minutes before introducing the next comic. When he got off stage, I hugged him again and told him what an honor it had been. I stayed and watched the rest of the show, which amounted to five more hours of Dave Chappelle with maybe thirty minutes of open mic comedy sprinkled in between. The fluidity of his thoughts, sometimes funny and sometimes not, was incredible to watch. He could make the simplest observation and it would cut through almost anything.

I thanked Chris Riggins, the producer of the show, for making a comedy dream come true. I went to my car, turned on the engine, and started crying tears of joy. I couldn't believe what had just happened.

I still can't!

# 13
# Assholisms

What is a microaggression? Psychologist Derald Wing Sue defines microaggressions as "brief, everyday exchanges that send denigrating messages to certain individuals because of their group membership." Examples include assuming that an Asian person is good at math, or talking about the one thing you know from African-American culture to the black person you just met. Microaggressions usually slip under the radar (that's why they're called "micro"). They can be a certain type of glance, a backhanded compliment—anything that takes you down a peg.

While the term was originally coined to describe this type of behavior towards people of color, it has since been adopted by other marginalized groups, including the Disability Community. I prefer to use a more straightforward term: *assholism*. Just to be clear, committing an assholism doesn't automatically make you an asshole. We all make mistakes trying to navigate this world of impossibly complicated interactions. I know I have been guilty of assholisms. What makes someone an asshole is when they know they're committing an assholism and choose to keep doing it.

It is also important to consider the varying degrees of assholisms. I try to grade them on a scale of one to ten. A one or two is something

I can give the benefit of the doubt. A nine or ten is something so fla-grant, so inflammatory that it merits a hefty "fuck you." Like Dante's nine circles of hell, the ten levels of assholism are all bad, but it's far better to be in the shallow end.

To give you an idea of how assholisms work, I've compiled some examples from my own life.

## "Is that Nina with Five Ns?"

Comedians tend to be more upfront with their assholisms. Maybe it's the informal setting or the pressure to have a snappy line on hand at all times. Whatever the reason, if a comedian makes an offhand remark about my stuttering, it will probably rank higher than aver-age on the assholometer. The upside is that I don't have to worry about coming up with a carefully measured response. I can just let them have it. These schlubs don't realize that they're actually giving me a precious gift: the ability to blow off thirty-something years of steam in a way that would get me in trouble anywhere else. Dealing with the brazen assholisms of comedy is good practice for dealing with the sneakier ones in civilian life.

One of the first assholisms I got from a comedian was at an open mic in San Francisco (Nick's Crispy Tacos, may it rest in peace). I was fairly new to the scene and didn't know anybody. Hoping to make some friends, I introduced myself to another comic, stuttering as usual on my name.

He quipped, "Is that Nina with five Ns?"

"No," I said, flipping him the double-bird, "it's Nina with two Ns!"

When it was my turn on stage, I delivered all my jokes about stut-tering in his direction, watching him squirm uncomfortably. Later that night, I went to a dive bar in Alameda to do another set. And who should I find there? Mr. Five Ns! He was very apologetic about the whole thing, and we have been on good terms ever since. Every now and then I'll still give him a hard time about it, especially since he considers himself a social justice type.

## Million Dollar Stutter

I was on an early morning talk show to promote my comedy troupe, The Comedians with Disabilities Act. As the segment wrapped and my interviewers threw back over to the anchor, the anchor said, "Tell [Nina] that Mel Tillis made a million dollars stuttering!" Obviously, this was intended in the good spirit of bland news banter. Or maybe he thought I would be inspired by the idea that you can receive a million dollars just for stuttering (show me the check and I will be!).

Measuring on the assholometer, I'd rate his comment as a five, maybe a six because of the public setting. Women who stutter are almost never on TV, apart from bikini-clad hot dog vendors and that woman on *Oprah* who became fluent in two minutes by wearing headphones (seriously, look it up). As a proud stutterer, I knew I had to say something.

When the anchor joked that Mel Tillis got a million dollars for stuttering, I calmly replied, "That and his talent." I think the anchor and the viewers got the message. I would say that my response was appropriately reserved for a level-six assholism.

I couldn't come at this guy guns blazing, like when I flipped off that other comedian with my "two Ns." The reporter had his fans and I was on his turf. Also, flipping the bird is not exactly morning show behavior (believe it or not, I do sometimes go the classy route). There is this balancing act of figuring out what will work in different situations. Who am I talking to? Do they have a "posse?" How will their posse respond? Who has the power? Will I come off as a privileged crybaby or the underdog?

As a comedian, I save my heaviest punches for punching up. When you have a David and Goliath power differential, there's no holding back. This wasn't one of those times. I was just politely reminding someone—and, more importantly, everyone watching at home—that we are more than our stuttering. We want to be seen for our abilities instead of our dysfluencies. The newscaster was able to understand that from my response without feeling attacked or humiliated.

In case you can't tell, I am very proud of the way I handled the situation. It's damn near impossible to come up with the perfect response to an uncomfortable situation on the spot, much less in a high-stakes environment like live television. When I walked off the set, my parents were waiting for me backstage.

"Good job with that one guy," my mom said. "And your hair looked really pretty!"

## From Mocking to Kissing

In 2011, I went to an NSA conference in Fort Worth, Texas. My friend Sasha suggested that it might be fun if I put on an all-stuttering comedy show. "Why not?" I thought. We scouted out a local dive bar, got the owner's blessing, and made it happen. The show featured an all-star, all-stuttering lineup consisting of myself, Jody Fuller, and Jason Walther. The crowd was unlike anything I'd ever seen, a Frankenstein hybrid of NSA-goers and local barflies, brought together by pure happenstance. One of the rowdier locals—let's call him Honky Tonk Hank—seemed like he might be a potential heckler, so I tried to nip things in the bud and talk to him before the show. Things were going well when my friend Pam Mertz showed up. Pam introduced herself and stuttered, prompting a loud cackle from Hank. She told him that his reaction (i.e. assholism) was "part of the problem," and proceeded to explain why. I left them to hash things out, knowing that Hank was in good hands. Pam hosts a podcast called "Women Who Stutter: Our Stories." If anyone was equipped to educate Hank, it was her.

By the time the show was over, Honky Tonk Hank was a changed man, presumably after many more drinks and interactions with the stuttering community. A drunken Hank said to me and Pam, "I want to French kiss one of you stutterers because, that would go on all night long." He wasn't being a smartass or trying to mock us; in the language of pervy old drunks, he was giving a compliment. Honky Tonk Hank ended up becoming my friend on Facebook. So did the bar, which was happy to have all that stuttering money coming in on a Thursday night. Disclaimer: stuttering money cashes the same as fluent money.

If you want to make progress, you have to get out in the world and interact with people you normally wouldn't interact with. Attitudes toward stuttering don't necessarily change because someone reads a tip sheet from a sensitivity workshop. Many times the tip sheet does more harm than good, turning stuttering into this weird thing that has to be explained, like the customs of an alien race on Star Trek or something. Sometimes all it takes is hanging out in a bar and talking, human to human. By engaging strangers in a social setting, we can change their attitudes from mockery to literally (and I assume passionately) wanting to kiss us. Assholisms can transform into many things, although I don't think old Hank got any takers that night.

## "The bravest thing I have ever seen."

Internet trolls love to post negative comments on my YouTube channel—so much that I've devoted an entire chapter of this book to them (good job, guys)! And yet, with so many online assholisms to choose from, the one I want to highlight was actually meant as a compliment.

"You doing stand-up comedy is the bravest thing I have ever seen!"

Uh… really?

I have a bit in my act where I break down this comment and illustrate the ridiculous logic behind it: "In your face 9/11 first responders! Who is braver, people who put their lives on the line, or me, the stuttering dick-joke-teller? Apparently me."

Sarcasm aside, describing what I do as "brave" trivializes the word. When you have people risking their own safety to help others, my actions are pretty damn small by comparison.

A woman once came up to me after a show and said, "You doing stand-up is the bravest thing I have ever seen! I mean, doing comedy is already brave, but when you add a stutter? Oh my God!" This person had no idea that she was acting out one of my bits almost word for word. Without missing a beat, Mean Dave chimed in, "Take that, 9/11 first responders!" She turned to him and said, "I know, right?" She was not being ironic.

Having a disability in our society is a surreal experience. When strangers aren't hurling insults, they're kissing our ass for no real reason—which is also an insult, because it's insincere and obvious and they expect us to believe it. It's *a very special* kind of assholism.

This happens all the time to my friend Michelle, who uses a wheelchair. She once had a job interview where the hiring manager said, "Michelle, you are an inspiration! You are a beacon of light in this world, and just meeting you has changed me." Holy crap, someone call the pope and tell him he's been replaced! Naturally, they didn't have room in their company for such a luminous being. I suppose it would be too much pressure to share a workspace with the second coming of Christ, especially if they had to invest in wheelchair-accessible file cabinets.

I realize that people who use words like "brave" and "inspiration" are mostly just trying to be nice. They hear these words in Hollywood movies and daytime talk shows, thinking that's how you're supposed to describe someone with disabilities. I can't just be a comedian. Michelle can't just be a psychologist at a job interview. According to them, we are first and foremost our disabilities…and that makes us heroes! Yeah, no thanks. If we're heroes for doing what everyone else does, we must be subject to some pretty low standards. Just talk to us like normal people. Hold us to the same standard. If I'm a hero, then so is everyone else. We're all just regular people taking life's lumps and doing what we can to make it work.

## "I get my shoes the same place you get yours"

This last story is different from the rest. It involves me and my friend Percy. Percy passed away several years ago, and I still miss him. He was blind and used a wheelchair due to a double leg amputation. Once, when we were working together on a presentation, he turned to me and said, "Do you notice something different about me?" Percy was pretty much bald, so I knew it wasn't a haircut. I examined him up and down.

"Oh my God!" I shouted. "Percy, you have legs!"

It was the first time I had seen him with his prosthetics. I had somehow managed to go all day without realizing that his dress slacks extended past the knee and down to his leather loafers! That was when I put my own foot in my mouth.

"Did the shoes come with the legs or did you have to buy them separately?"

If only I had stuttered on the question, it might have given me a few extra seconds to realize how stupid it was!

"Now Nina," Percy said gently, "I get my shoes the same place you get yours."

"I know! I know! I don't know why I said that!"

I acknowledged my mistake and we moved on. In these types of situations, the important thing is to have humility. Being humble not only helps you save face; it shows the other person that you hear them. Percy was able to help me recognize my mistake. By taking the time to correct me, he showed that he was invested in our friendship.

Assholisms don't have to drive us apart. We can take annoying comments—like mine about the shoes—and use them to develop a better understanding of each other. Of course, it's not always clear how to do that. How do we bring attention to something that makes us uncomfortable? Are we willing to have those conversations with each other? I hope so.

The only way to understand another person is by listening to them. And I mean REALLY listening. Not active listening, where we take what the other person said and pitch it back to them with our own spin. We need to listen with heart and humility. We need to absorb what the other person is saying and let their experience change us. Let it change the way we think and act.

This kind of listening doesn't come naturally to most people. It takes learning and practice to accept someone else's point of view without immediately relating it back to yourself. I get this a lot when I perform as a storyteller in Berkeley, AKA the Bay Area capital of political correctness. People will come up after the show and assure me that *they* don't do any of the rude things I talk about. Okay, great! Am I supposed to pin a medal on them for not being rude? We are all capable of assholisms like the people I describe in this chapter, including myself. We all make mistakes. Personally, I welcome those mistakes, and not just because they give me material for my act (though that doesn't hurt!). I believe these mistakes are the key to personal growth. If you open up and learn to confront the discomfort, you can turn every regrettable interaction into an opportunity to improve yourself, your relationships, and the world around you.

# 14
# Stuttersplain

I've noticed that many able-bodied people possess a miraculous superpower: whenever they are in the presence of someone with a disability, they are suddenly endowed with expert knowledge of said disability.

"Oh, you have multiple sclerosis? Have you considered going gluten free?"

"I bet if you pray hard enough, the Good Lord will heal your cerebral palsy. Can I pray for you?" Note: this is usually followed by disappointment when the person being prayed for doesn't come flying out of their wheelchair.

People who stutter are no less immune to the "help" of these self-appointed experts. Consider the following anecdote: I was with my friend Michelle, having a casual (and private) conversation at Starbucks. Michelle has rheumatoid arthritis and, as I mentioned, uses a wheelchair. As for me, I was stuttering up a storm. So when this guy started glancing over at us, I figured there were two possible explanations: either we were so smokin' hot that he couldn't keep his eyes off us, or he was itching to share a secret cure to one of our conditions. Unfortunately, it turned out to be the latter.

He approached us and began the awkward preamble to his spiel.

I gritted my teeth and waited to see if it would be aimed at me or Michelle. I guess it was my lucky day, because he started to dispense with the free elocution lessons. His advice was the usual "just breathe," "slow down and think about what you are saying" sort of crap. I thanked him for the free advice with an implied "now get the hell out of my face," but he still lingered. Maybe he was waiting for me to bow down and kiss his feet in humble gratitude. When we finally got rid of him, Michelle was in disbelief.

"Oh my God!" she exclaimed. "For once, I wasn't the freak!"

Michelle spent most of her time around able-bodied people, so she was used to being the odd one out. Never before had she seen someone practically climb over her wheelchair to offer useless advice on someone else's disability.

What we witnessed that day is a phenomenon I like to call *stuttersplaining*.

Maybe you've heard of mansplaining, when a man explains women's issues to a woman. It might be intended as a show of compassion or allyship, but it usually comes off as patronizing and/or belittling. Just like mansplaining, stuttersplaining occurs when someone who has never experienced a particular issue decides to lecture about it to someone who lives with that issue every day. Stuttersplaining is a type of assholism, but it is so prevalent and wide-ranging that I need a whole other chapter just to 'splain it.

Unlike mansplainers, stuttersplainers can be any gender. They can be any color, any religion, any sexual orientation—all they have to be is fluent and offering unsolicited advice to a person who stutters. The one predictor for stuttersplaining seems to be personality: aggressive types who enjoy sticking their nose in other people's business are more likely to stick their nose in someone else's disability. They lack the humility to consider that their immediate take on an issue might have already occurred to someone who has dealt with it their entire life.

Don't get me wrong, I want people to feel comfortable talking about stuttering. We *need* to talk about stuttering! But here's the thing—unless I bring it up, I'd like to stick to the discussion at hand and not derail into awkward tangents about my speech. In other words, if I want advice on taking psychedelic mushrooms to cure my stutter, I will ask for it!

Consider this an open guide to stuttersplaining. Although it takes on many forms, the underlying cause is always the same: people not minding their own damn business! As you read through the following examples, imagine having to deal with this stuff on a regular basis. Bleh!

## The TV Told Me

Stuttersplainers often like to back up their advice with citations. These include "I was watching Dr. Oz," "Did you see on Oprah," "I have a friend who," and other hit classics. When a stutterer hears any of these phrases, we instinctively clench our various body parts and prepare for the pain. My personal favorite is, "So I heard on NPR." A graduate student once came up to me after I had finished leading a workshop on disability awareness. His opener: "So I was watching NPR . . ." (first of all, how do you watch National Public Radio?). He went on to explain that "stutterers don't stutter when they talk to animals, so could there be something there with that?" He speculated that dogs might be used to help stutterers become fluent. In my most nurturing and educational tone, I suggested that people who stutter enjoy the company of animals because they shut the hell up and let us talk. Personally, I've never had a dog try to finish my sentence for me.

Another time I was approached at a different workshop by a different graduate student with a different question: "Why can't you stop stuttering like the guy in *The King's Speech*?" For the record, I enjoyed the movie and applaud it for bringing stuttering awareness to the general movie-going public. It's always great when a stutterer is portrayed on screen and doesn't kill anyone or get killed. Not only that, it's a good movie! Still, there are many nuances in the film that people seemed to have overlooked, like the fact that HE STILL STUTTERED AT THE END OF THE MOVIE! Seriously. The king gave one speech kind of fluently. When his elocution coach points out that he still stuttered on the Ws, he responds, "Well, I had to throw in a few so they knew it was me." Keeping it real, King George!

I pointed this out to the graduate student in the workshop, once again adopting my most nurturing teaching voice. I explained how a fluent person's interpretation of the film might vary from that of a person who stutters. I talked about the need to address discrimination and welcome different communication styles in our society. He responded with, "Yeah, but can't you do some of those tricks, like the one where he stands on his toes?" I was about to say, "Or the one where he starts cussing, because I'd like to try that right about now!"

## Hippies and Jesus Freaks

When the media isn't inspiring people to fix us, there's always good old religion. It's not unusual for people with disabilities to encounter strangers wanting to lay hands on them and pray for a cure that will be a manifestation of God's greatness (doesn't that sound fun?). In regard to stuttering, I never understood why God would give me a stutter only to take it away through the power of some guy with sweaty palms shouting at the top of his lungs. This dude is supposed to help me with my speech? He's the one speaking in tongues!

Whenever someone brings up the topic of divine healing, I like to point out that Moses stuttered (true). Instead of curing him of his stutter, God suggested that Moses have his brother Aaron speak for him—the earliest Judeo-Christian example of an accommodation! So, if someone ever tries to pray for your fluency, you can tell them: "God didn't cure Moses' stutter; he's probably not worried about mine." And yes, I have totally used that line on people.

I live in the San Francisco Bay Area, where people claim to be "spiritual" instead of religious. I might not have God's healing hands laid on me, but plenty of New Age hippies, yuppies, and yippies have their own magical prescriptions for fluency. I met my first hippie stuttersplainer in Calistoga, land of the hot spring and mud bath. My family has been going there for generations. Before it was converted into a resort town for the Whole Foods demographic, Calistoga used to be a quaint vacation spot favored by working class Italians and Eastern European Jews in Northern California. I can still hear the old women yelling at me and my brother for splashing in the pool, afraid we'd ruin their meticulous bouffants.

As I got older and more comfortable with the idea of being touched by a stranger, I began to take advantage of the town's many massage therapists. Whenever they asked which parts of my body needed special attention, I would always request my jaw. It's easily my most overworked muscle (too bad I can't say the same for my stomach or butt cheeks). One massage therapist—let's call her Hippy Dippy Pippy—asked if I suffered from TMJ (Temporomandibular Joint Disorder). I told her that I stutter and it causes a lot of tension in my jaw area. Big mistake. Pippy began to unload all her magical fairy-dust on me, dreaming up speech therapy techniques that involved hempseed oil and looking at rainbows. Hoping these rambles would result in extra massage time, I decided to humor her. At one point she asked, "Do you stutter when you sing?"

"Nope," I said. "Singing engages a different part of the brain that isn't affected by stuttering."

"Well, singing is good for the soul," Pippy said, glossing over my scientific explanation entirely. "You need to sing! That will help you!"

If singing cures stuttering because it's good for the soul, then I guess I stutter because there's something wrong with my soul. What bad karma did I earn in a previous life to make me talk like this? Mel Tillis and Bill Withers both stutter, and they are singers. Their souls must be totally out of whack, because not even their beautiful voices and lyrics can make them fluent. Oh, their tarnished souls!

These "helpful tips" from strangers might seem well-meaning on the surface, but there's a subtle hostility running underneath. Their desire to fix us implies that we are broken, that the way we talk isn't acceptable and we need to do something differently. Whether it's someone telling my friend to put a live canary in his mouth (seriously), or *American Idol* judges telling a stuttering contestant to "just sing instead of talk," these suggestions will never be helpful. If someone wants quack advice on how to get rid of a stutter, they are free to seek it out—most likely on the Internet—but unless they specifically ask you for help, please keep your remedies to yourself. Stuttering is a complex speech style (note how I didn't say disorder). It is impacted by many factors that vary from individual to individual. If there ever is a "cure" for stuttering, it's not going to be discovered by our friend Pippy during a five-minute chat on a massage table. But even if these people had degrees in speech pathology, that wouldn't make their unsolicited advice any less rude. We don't expect physicians to walk up to random people and tell them they're overweight. Why should it be any different for people who stutter?

## Magical Sex

A while back, I was promoting one of my upcoming gigs on a Sunday morning radio show. Things were going more or less according to plan, until we started taking calls. What is it about AM radio that brings the weirdos out of the woodwork? Especially the call-in segments. It's like a garage sale for opinions: most of it is regular stuff, but every now and then you find one that makes you go, "WTF?" That morning we got a prime example of WTF, when a listener called to tell us about her friend who "found true love and doesn't stutter anymore."

I was polite on the air, but I couldn't stop laughing about it with my friends after. That poor woman! She was a grown adult who still believed in Disney princess magic. Who knew that I've been a passive Stuttering Beauty this whole time, waiting for a prince to come and break the spell?

That caller and her "true love" theory did a great job of showing how misogyny hurts us all. Her fairytale logic not only undermines the autonomy of women; it insults my husband as well. Ethan and I have been married for a while now, and I still stutter. I guess he isn't my true love? Thanks for nothing, Ethan! My stuttering is all your fault. That, and the window blinds you broke in the living room.

While it's easy to make fun of the caller and her delusions, she is far from alone. A surprising number of people believe that stuttering is caused by a lack of romantic/sexual fulfillment. Once, after a stand-up show, I had a male audience member offer his own diagnosis: "You stutter because you're having the wrong orgasms." I guess he missed the part of my act where I humiliate guys who say pervy shit. When I asked him what would constitute the "right" orgasms, he simply replied, "In the ass." Wow. Believe it or not, he had three women in his party (and zero qualms about acting creepy in front of them). Clearly embarrassed by their association with this guy and his rapey comment, the women put him in his place. "Did you even hear her jokes?" one of them said. "That's the kind of thing she was talking about," said another. "Now she's going to make fun of your dumb ass on stage!" With all that having been said, I simply added that there is no correlation between stuttering and sexual intercourse.

They couldn't be farther apart in tone, but "true love" and "in the ass" both have something in common. Do you know what it is? Take a moment and guess (hint: it's Freud's favorite answer for everything).

Did you guess yet? No?

Don't make me say it.

PENIS!

Both of these stories revolve around people who believe in the same patriarchal dick-cures-everything bullshit. We can be saved by accepting Penis as our personal savior! And not just women. The myth can be modified for men who stutter, in which they are miraculously cured by having their penises touched in the right way. Consider the 1975 academy award-winning film, *One Flew Over the Cuckoo's Nest*. At one point in the movie, the stuttering character Billy Bibbit becomes temporarily fluent after losing his virginity to a woman named Candy. Of course, no actual professional would ever prescribe such treatment.

. . . right?

I was talking to my friend Virgil, a young man who stutters. Our conversation turned to the subject of relationships, which turned to me speaking openly about sex, because I'm a liberated woman who survived Catholic school and that's how I roll. I think my openness put Virgil at ease, because he shared the fact that he was a virgin. He didn't have a strict religion or any sexual hang-ups; it just hadn't happened yet. He'd been on several dates and probably could have gotten laid just to get it over with, but that's not what he wanted. And besides, he was only 23. There was still plenty of time.

Then Virgil told me something else: "My therapist says once I have sex, I'll stop stuttering."

"WHAT?!"

My eyeballs nearly shot out of my head and hit Virgil in the face. I fought back the urge to tell him what I thought of his so-called therapist and followed up with a neutral question: "How do you feel about that?"

Virgil said he knew it was bullshit, but his therapist had helped him in other ways, so he let it slide.

"Good," I said. "Because you know that's fucked up, right?"

I don't know where Virgil's therapist got the idea that virginity causes stuttering, but I would bet my money on *One Flew Over the Cuckoo's Nest*. It wouldn't be the first time that a mental health professional ignored scientific literature and based their opinion on a movie. My friend Pam once had a therapist tell her that stuttering is caused by emotional trauma, because "that's what they said in *The King's Speech*." This is literally as stupid as a marine biologist basing all their knowledge on *Jaws*. Stupider, actually, because the characters in *The King's Speech* are working with 1930s science. At least *Jaws* happened in the 70s.

Over the next couple of weeks, Virgil and I would joke about what his therapist had said. But I was still pissed off! For most people, losing your virginity is an overload of expectations, anxieties, emotions.... what kind of sociopath would add an imaginary cure for stuttering on top of all that?! I was angry to the point that I was ready to devirginize Virgil myself, just to prove that asshole therapist wrong. But then the rational side of my brain won out.

Virgil eventually did meet that special someone. As they grew closer, I knew nature would soon take its course. Then one morning I got a text.

"I still stutter."

I immediately texted back.

"Keep trying for a cure! ;-)"

# 15
# Stutter Like a Girl

People who stutter make up one percent of the adult population. Women who stutter make up one quarter of one percent. That is one in four hundred people! We are the rarest kind of unicorn. Pooping-rainbows-while-doing-the-Macarena-level-of-rare unicorns. While it's fun to think of myself belonging to an exclusive club, it makes it that much harder to find other unicorns I can relate to. Much of my life has been a search for people who understand me. When I finally found my stuttering sisters, the whole game changed.

The first time I met another stuttering unicorn was in middle school. This other girl—we'll call her Elizabeth—was in my class, which is statistically comparable to being hit by lightning on a roller coaster. She was the same girl who laughed at me at the inauguration rehearsal. Like many people with disabilities, Elizabeth and I never talked about our common experience. I never said to her, "I know why you talk like a valley girl and say 'like' all the time." She never said to me, "I know you act weird to cover up your stuttering." We shared the same secret, but without any space to talk about it. Instead of finding friendship and community, we drowned in isolation and shame.

I recently dug up my old seventh grade diary. Within those

pencil-doodled pages, I express my dislike for Elizabeth and how her "studering [sic] is even worse than mine." Another page shows me keeping a tally of all the times she stuttered while reading out loud in class. I guess you could say I was projecting my insecurities. After she laughed at me during our inauguration rehearsal, I was ready to return the favor—at least in my private ruminations.

My speech therapist Elaine understood the importance of peer interaction among people who stutter, especially teens and young adults. When I was in eighth grade, she set me up on a playdate with another unicorn my age. I was overjoyed. Unlike Elizabeth, this new girl would be cool and nice and we would have so much in common! We would meet and discover we were stuttering soulmates and become the dysfluent Laverne and Shirley. And then we would call each other every day and talk about who made fun of us and how they were stupid jerks. And then, during school breaks our families would vacation at the same hotel, and we could hang out all day at the pool. And then! And then we would walk to the nearby frozen yogurt stand where we would both stutter on "Reese's Pieces" when we ordered our toppings. The possibilities were endless! As I got ready for therapy, I treated it like a first date. I changed out of my Catholic School uniform and into the cool kid clothes I bought from the Esprit Outlet in San Francisco. Decked out in my leggings and oversized sweatshirt with geometrical designs (it was the 80s), I was off to meet my new stuttering BFF!

And then I met her. We'll call her Susie. As soon as I walked into the room, I got the feeling that Susie might be a little on the snooty side. She was from an upscale neighborhood in San Ramon, a cut above my family's working class background. She wore her shirt collar up with a preppy sweater draped around her neck, pink topsider shoes to complete the look. I mean, I only wore topsiders because they were one of three shoes sanctioned by my school dress code, and those had to be brown. Pink topsiders? Did this girl think she was about to enter a yacht regatta? My suspicions of snobbery were confirmed when she started complaining how Sutter Street in San Francisco sounds too much like "Stutter Street," which triggered her. Yeesh! If she hated things that reminded her of stuttering, how was she going to handle hanging out with me?

Things looked grim, but I wasn't going to let Susie's preppy clothes and attitude get in the way of our friendship. We were still destined to become the stuttering Mary and Rhoda!

Or not. After our awkward introduction, I tried following up with a phone call. Susie was cold and short with me, clearly in a hurry to hang up and get back to her badminton lessons or whatever people with sweaters around their neck do for fun. I guess it wasn't going to work out after all. Our stuttering sisterhood wasn't enough to overcome class differences and how we wore our collared shirts. Or maybe it was because we were ashamed of our stuttering, and we saw our own insecurities reflected in each other. Or maybe it was my shoes?

When I was growing up, there were no support groups for children and teens who stutter. Thankfully, things have changed. Organizations like FRIENDS, SAY, and the NSA organize youth events that focus on self-acceptance and community. They provide a space for children to examine their feelings without shame or fear of being judged. They also let the kids have fun, which is equally important! I wish the younger me had those kinds of opportunities. I am grateful to Elaine for setting me up on that playdate, even if the chemistry fizzled out. She understood the importance of kids having friends who don't make them feel different. Many years later, I learned that Elaine's husband is one of the founding members of the organization that has now become the NSA. She knew the importance of a stuttering community because she saw it in her own backyard.

As important as Elaine and the NSA were to my development, I still wish I'd had a stuttering female role model when I was younger.

Someone to give me an idea of the woman I might grow up to be (bikini hot dog vendors aside). I didn't have that experience until I was in my thirties at the 2009 NSA conference. I will never forget the feeling of suddenly discovering my unicorn tribe! For the first time ever, I was able to socialize with my own gender and not be the one who sounds different. That's a given if you're fluent, but imagine how mind-blowing it would be to have that experience for the first time as an adult.

I met so many amazing women at that conference, but there was one encounter that was truly incredible. About five years earlier, I was counseling a student who stuttered. We'll call her Sheila. Sheila required social services and I had to refer her to a local shelter. When I called the homeless shelter to check on her, the woman answering the phone got confused and thought I was Sheila, because of my stuttering. I immediately went into defense mode. What, do we all sound the same? Does this lady think anyone who stutters must be a "patient" and not someone of authority? Of course I kept these thoughts to myself, maintaining a professional tone.

That's when the woman on the phone said, "I stutter too." Could it be? Three unicorns brought together by pure coincidence? A stuttering trifecta? Statistically, it felt like winning the Powerball Lotto (financially, not so much). I fought back the urge to enagage in personal conversation and kept things strictly professional. I could hear the disappointment in her young, stuttering voice as I resisted her own attempts to socialize. If only she knew how badly I wanted to invite her out for lunch and pedicures! I wanted to get that frozen yogurt with Reese's Pieces I had been craving for the last twenty years! But I didn't do any of that. I ignored my personal feelings and stuck to the business at hand, which was taking care of Sheila. That being said, I was able to gather a few details about this mystery woman. I learned that her name was Kristel and that she was considering a master's degree in counseling.

I spoke to Kristel a few more times on the phone, always in a professional context. Once Sheila left the center, however, our relationship was no longer bound by the duties of my job. I called her back and left a message: "Hi Kristel, this is Nina. I just wanted to invite you to call me if you had any questions about graduate school and stuttering, or the field of counseling and psychology. I would love to talk to you about it!"

I waited for her to call me back so we could get lunch and mani-pedis and finally become the stuttering Laverne and Shirley. But that call never came. My emotional distance in our previous conversations must have pushed her away.

So now, five years later, I was at this conference in Arizona, hanging out with a group of women in the hotel wine bar. I started chatting with one of them, a young, blonde woman from Farmingdale, New York. When I said I was from Oakland, her eyes lit up.

"I spent some time there and loved it!"

She went on to explain how she had an internship with Catholic Charities and used to volunteer at a shelter. That's when we both realized who the other person was. The woman on the phone!

"I always wondered what happened to you!" I screamed, unable to contain my excitement.

We immediately hugged and started filling in each other's backstories, which turned out to have a lot of common ground. We both had multiple disability experiences (her with cerebral palsy and me with my learning disability). We both had parents with disabilities (her dad stutters and my dad is hard-of-hearing). And we both yearned to connect with other women who stutter!

If women who stutter make up one quarter of one percent of the adult population, that means the chances of meeting a unicorn are 1/400. That means the chances of meeting the same unicorn after a missed connection are what, one in a billion? I have dyslexia and a hell of a time with word problems, but that sounds about right,

right? The odds have got to be on par with spotting an actual, rainbow-pooping unicorn in the wild.

Unlike Elizabeth in my seventh grade class, or Susie with her pink topsider shoes, I knew Kristel would be a friend for life, despite the physical distance. Whenever she and her husband come to San Francisco, we always go out for dinner at Golden Boy Pizza. Whenever Ethan and I go to New York, we always sleep on an air mattress in their living room. Kristel even hooked me up with a speaking gig at the place where she works: The American Institute on Stuttering!

Spending time with Kristel and the other women at that conference changed my life. Many of them were younger than me, but in a lot of ways I was their junior. They retroactively served as the stuttering female role models I never had as a kid. Without those role models, growing up was like trying to assemble a puzzle without seeing the picture on the box. I had to imagine my own picture of what it means to be a woman who stutters—a picture distorted by teenage insecurities and the media/consumer culture that preys on them. Meeting all these awesome, self-actualized women helped me see the picture I was meant to be working toward all this time. Because of them, I started to rearrange the puzzle pieces in my life and make something better.

# 16
# The Week of Invasive Brain Surgeries

A stranger once suggested that I try invasive brain surgery for my stuttering. A few days later, someone else offered me the exact same advice! Have you ever had one of those weeks where everyone wants you to undergo a risky and expensive medical procedure so they don't have to wait an extra five seconds for you to finish a sentence? No? Just me?

Something tells me this was more than coincidence. I don't think the alignment of Venus and Saturn can explain two separate people approaching me with the same wacky idea over the course of a few days. My guess is that it had something to do with the news cycle that week. At the time, there were a lot of puff pieces about a supposed "miracle treatment" for Parkinson's Disease, which involved (surprise) surgical brain implants! Could it be that these two people saw the same news clip and viewed me as the perfect opportunity to share their newfound knowledge? Or maybe it was Venus and Saturn.

The first "brain comment" happened at a corporate training conference. I was there to give a keynote on disability access and learning disabilities. After my presentation, I sat and had lunch with some of the employees. One of them, the guy sitting closest to me, steered the conversation towards stuttering (mine in particular). After dispensing with the usual FAQs, he asked me a question I hadn't heard before:

"Is there an invasive brain surgery that could help you not stutter?"

"Stuttering comes from a pathway in the frontal lobe," I said. "I don't think I'd be comfortable with a frontal lobotomy."

He accepted my answer and moved on.

The second brain comment happened at a comedy show in San Francisco. I won't dress it up for you—it was a shit gig. There were only five people in the audience, which makes a performer feel less like a respectable adult and more like a child putting on a play for their parents in the living room. A bad show can still be an opportunity to have fun and hang out with your friends, but I wasn't really friends with anyone on the lineup, so that was out.

About halfway through the show, I went outside to get a break from the stuffy air and stale jokes. Another comedian was standing out there, presumably doing the same thing (only with a cigarette). We didn't know each other well, but she had seen my act enough times to know that I stutter and have no interest in changing that fact. Still, she felt compelled to share a possible lead on a cure.

"I was just watching this news thing on Parkinson's," she began. "They have this invasive brain surgery where they implant something that helps the patient. Can't they do that for your stuttering?"

Fresh off the last brain comment, I fell back on my old line about the frontal lobotomy—minus the fake smile this time, because I was standing outside a bar and not sitting in a corporate cafeteria.

"Well I thought it might help," she said with a bored look on her face. She threw her cigarette on the ground and walked back inside.

During that week of invasive brain surgeries, I learned more about my personal boundaries and where they lie. With the person who made the second brain surgery comment, I was at a crappy show and not getting paid for it, so my patience was understandably thinner. I was already wasting my time on a useless gig, and I wasn't in the mood to waste even more time explaining neuroscience to a comedian I hardly knew.

It's like when my friend Gina and her black stuttering friends got interrupted by a white guy at a stuttering conference. They all had just met and were getting to know each other. He came up to them and said, "Gee, it must be hard to stutter *and* be black!" That was their cue to drop everything and initiate this brave cultural emissary into the secret world of stuttering while black, all so that he could go back to his other white friends and wow them with his newly acquired wokeness. Gina and her new friends had just met, and suddenly they have to put all that on hold (during happy hour, no less) to explain intersectionality to *this* guy?

There is a time and a place. If that guy wanted to learn about the black stuttering experience, he could have referred to a number of discussion panels, kiosks, information booths, and other resources provided by the conference. If he was feeling especially studious, he might look up the works of Dr. Derek Eugene Daniels, a professor at Wayne State University who wrote his entire master thesis on the black stuttering experience (see: Google). The point is, don't go looking for answers in a bar from a group of friends that doesn't include you . . . and then not even offer to buy them a round of drinks!

People have the right to choose where, when, and with whom they have these conversations. With the person who made the first brain surgery comment, I had just given a presentation on disability issues as part of a week-long conference. I was being paid to train him and everyone else there. Helping him reach a better understanding of stuttering in that context seemed appropriate. Also, the swanky hotel accommodations had me in a good mood: Ethan and I had a room overlooking Asilomar State Beach.

Ethan enjoyed the accommodations very much. In fact, when

that guy at the lunch table asked me his question about brain surgery, Ethan was sitting right there with us (to cash in on that free food, of course). He listened quietly to the conversation, choosing not to intervene. He made the right call; I wanted to handle this one on my own. Later, when we were alone, he said something to the effect of, "What the fuck was that? Brain surgery for your stutter?" I was thankful to have him there, to share a cathartic laugh and assure me that I wasn't the only one who found the situation uncomfortable. Many times that validation is all it takes to move on from an unpleasant experience. I can't tell you how many times I've heard, "Oh, they didn't mean it like *that*," or "You're just being oversensitive." People who pass for society's definition of normal can easily dismiss the weird shit that happens to people who don't, because of course it never happens to them. As for the rest of us, when weird shit happens (and it will), it's nice to have others recognize it.

Life is like YouTube: the more you put yourself out there, the more you will get unwanted comments (more on that in a second). Still, I'll take invasive questions over invasive brain implants any day, if that is what it takes to be myself and not some surgically corrected version of normal. Of course, I would love to be myself without having to deal with invasive questions, but the world isn't there yet.

# 17

# How to Have a YouTube Account Without Turning Your Brain into a Public Toilet

I have over 1,500,000 views on my YouTube channel. Most of the videos are relatively lightweight, with only a few hundred views and a handful of comments each. These are usually the ones where I talk directly to the camera, answering questions from a middle school kid or telling quick jokes—how many disabled people does it take to screw in a lightbulb? (One to screw it in and five able-bodied people to say what an inspiration they are.) Then there are the middleweight entries, netting anywhere between 5,000 and 45,000 views. Examples from this category include, "Shit People Say to People Who Stutter," footage from a Mel Tillis press conference, and snippets from my live performances. Finally, we come to the heavyweight champion of my YouTube channel, weighing in at over one million views: my first heckler video.

When I first began stand-up, I would always hear stories of this or that heckler video going viral and grabbing a million views off YouTube. I don't know why, but people love heckler videos. Maybe it has something to do with our conflict-oriented culture? People want to see blood! In any case, I wanted a piece of the action. As a new comic determined to establish a name for myself, I decided one night to make my own heckler video. Now, that wasn't my intention going into the show; my original plan was only to film my set at the Purple Onion. But as the night went on, the prospect of getting a usable clip seemed less and less likely, thanks to this one bozo who wouldn't shut up. The heckler, who identified himself as "Devin," had been ruining every single act with his drunken outbursts. Any other club would have tossed him to the curb, but the Purple Onion—under this iteration of management—was all too happy to keep pouring gas on the fire as long as they could charge it to Devin's tab.

I decided to shift tactics. Time to make a heckler video! Instead of doing a regular set, I would bait Devin into a verbal cage match. As an added twist, my parents were also in the audience, sitting between Devin and the stage. Few things annoy my mom like public drunkenness and attention seekers, so I knew she was approaching peak levels of pissed off. If Devin were to say or do anything disrespectful towards me, that would be the final straw. All I had to do was light a match and watch the fireworks.

I got on stage and told Devin that my mom and dad were in the front row, waiting to kick his ass if he got out of line (angry Italian parents of a daughter with disabilities and whatnot). Then I told my joke about the guy asking for the rest of my sentence and me asking where the rest of his dick is. Only this time I personalized it: "Where's the rest, Devin?"

(Just as a disclaimer, I have since moved on from insults about small penises. Body shaming is uncool and there are better ways to insult insecure men. I've grown beyond small dick jokes. I'm bigger than that.)

The rest of my set went exactly as planned. I got to destroy a heckler on camera and I got my million-plus views. When I posted the video online, I received my first negative YouTube comment. Then another. And another. I was stunned. What kind of person takes time out of their day to insult a stranger they will never meet? The video wasn't my best work as a comic, but I wanted to show the perspective of an adult with a disability pushing back (and I wanted that juicy view count!). Well, I got my views, and I learned that they come with a price. As the clicks piled on, so did the insults. Common themes include a) women not being funny, b) how my breasts look, and c) prescribing dank weed to cure my stuttering. Connecting these three data points, I'm guessing that the majority of my trolls are grown men who wear flame-decal bowling shirts and subscribe to the Spencer's Gifts catalog.

While most of the comments are just plain awful, I have to give credit to the ones that are actually funny. I always give points for creativity and hilarity, even if I'm the punchline. These are my top ten:

1. "She'd be an inspiration if she were funny." -- my personal favorite.

2. "Saying that she's not funny after hearing three minutes of her act would be like me deciding that you're an asshole after only reading your seven word comment. However, I will say that you are only one or two words away from being a confirmed asshole!" – not directed at me, but another commenter who wrote, "She's not funny."

3. "About as funny as a kick in the balls, stutter or no stutter." – my male friends argue that a kick in the balls is hysterical (depending on whose balls).

4. "Nina, I just want to say you are a cunt-cunt-cunt-continuing source of inspiration." – I hear this is stolen from *South Park*, which explains why it's funny.

5. "Stuttering? More like sluttering!"

6. "I have meat in my refrigerator funnier than she is."

7. "Well I thought you were pretty damn funny, I love the way you make the stutter work into your routine. That being said, I'd love to show you my penis."

I know I said top ten, but seven is all I can manage without getting depressed.

Anyone with an online presence is liable to get this kind of treatment, thanks to the army of anonymous trolls that pollute the Internet. YouTubers get trolled with comments. Businesses get trolled on Yelp. Even academics get trolled on sites like RateMyProfessor. com. Howard Stern says he temporarily deleted his Twitter account because even he couldn't stomach all the toxic commentary.

I am a woman with a disability operating in a space typically reserved for able-bodied men. I always knew there would be push-back, but nothing could have prepared me for the sheer number of trolls out there. One after another, they came to anonymously unload their diseased mental waste. My brain had become a public bathroom! A disgusting, graffiti-on-the-stalls, backed-up-toilet gas station bathroom! If I didn't want to disable the comment feature altogether (I didn't), I would have to mentally distance myself from that horror show.

I think it's important that people share their stories on the Internet. Unlike television, which is brokered through executive bias, the Internet provides a platform where anyone can make their voice heard. Unfortunately, many of those voices are loud, hateful, and determined to drown out everyone else.

Don't let them!

The Internet needs your passion, creativity, and ideas. I can't stand the thought of people being discouraged from doing what they love because some asshole bullied them online. There are ways of dealing

with cyberbullies, as I have learned (the hard way) from my experience on YouTube. And now I am going to share those lessons with
you. Consider me your instructor in defense against the troll arts. I
hope you never encounter any of these mythical monsters, but if you
do, at least you'll be more prepared than I was.

## Know Your Boundaries

Before you get caught in a troll attack with no plan, take the time to
answer some questions for yourself. What am I willing to do or not do
online? What lines am I willing to cross with my own behavior? What
lines am I not willing to cross or have others cross? Consider different
scenarios and decide which comments you will engage, which comments you will delete, and when you will need to unplug and take a
break from it all. Having these rules in place ahead of time will make
it easier to think clearly if you ever get hit by a roving band of trolls.

Here are some examples of my own boundaries: If someone posts
a comment insulting me, fine; if they post a comment insulting my
friends or anyone else in my videos, I will delete the shit out of it! If
someone leaves a hateful comment, I won't respond to it. If someone
leaves a supportive comment, sadly, I won't respond to that either
(trolls love to jump on any kind of positive interaction and poison
it with their bile). I don't respond to comments at all, with one big
exception—if someone is spreading misinformation about stuttering.

I have to say something in that case. People are entitled to their
asshole opinions, but facts need to be upheld. Like when someone
said that my stutter is fake because I have a confident stage presence
and stuttering is caused by a lack of confidence. When I read ignorant shit like this, I have an obligation to set the record straight. I
never persuade the author of the comment to change their mind, but
at least people reading it will know what's what. Spreading the truth
is more important than winning any argument.

I also have my boundaries in stand-up. A few years back, I was

on a campaign to educate people about the word "retard." I personally hate the word, as does most of the Disabled Community. Some
comedians have been able to do bits about the word and pull it off,
but most are just Lenny Bruce wannabes trying to be edgy. It's not
important if people with intellectual disabilities say the word hurts
them; apparently they matter less than getting cheap laughs in a bar
or Ann Coulter profiting from her latest book of hate speech. I tried
addressing my feelings about the word on stage, but it just made me
so damn angry. I guess some demons are too powerful to be exor-
cised through comedy. So I choose to set a boundary for myself and
not engage in that particular topic on stage.

Knowing when to engage and disengage is also useful in social
situations. Sometimes, in a group conversation, I feel like a crossing
guard at a dangerous intersection. If I sense that someone is about
to say something that will make everyone uncomfortable, I try to
steer the conversation in another direction. If I'm unsuccessful, I feel
partly to blame for the other person's gaffe. How's that for codependency? So I have to set hard boundaries for myself and fight the urge
to play traffic controller. If someone wants to say something offensive,
it's not my job to save them from embarrassing themselves. I will
probably have to address it after the fact, but I'm not liable for what
other people say.

If I catch someone make an assholism, I usually point it out by
making fun of them. But should I do that on YouTube? With all my
haters? That's a full time job! Forget it, my energy is better spent elsewhere. Knowing your boundaries will help you reaffirm your prior-
ities. Focus on what you want to accomplish and don't let the haters
derail you from your true mission.

## Know Who You Are

If you are going to publish anything, be ready for people to challenge
you. When I wrote my first book, some people objected to my use of

the phrase, "Disabled person," instead of "person with disabilities." Still, I didn't regret my choice of words. My words are connected to my thoughts, and my thoughts are part of who I am. I also know who I'm speaking for, which is primarily myself. I don't speak for everyone who stutters or everyone who has a disability. I definitely don't speak for communities and cultures that I don't belong to. I know who I am, and that knowledge keeps me grounded.

Knowing who you are and where you stand will strengthen your ideas. It will protect you against the corrosive effects of trolling. When the trolls tell me that "women aren't funny," I know they are wrong. When they tell me that "people who stutter shouldn't do comedy," I know they are wrong. When they tell me that my speech is "nothing a little dank maryjane can't fix," I know they are wrong. Why? Because they don't know me. But I know me. I know I love comedy, I know my own stuttering experience, and I know that pot brownies just make me paranoid.

## Think of the Bigger Picture

Even the most innocent content can make you a target for online abuse. You could share a recipe for lentils on your blog and have someone call you a dumb c-word for using olive oil instead of coconut oil. Don't think for a second that it reflects on you. These empty and hateful words float around the Internet like airborne germs, and sometimes you randomly catch them. You have to develop a mental immune system to keep the bullies from infecting your self-esteem. It helps that Internet trolls come with their own built-in quarantine, since they're fully contained in your screen. The more you engage in life outside your computer/mobile device, the more their words shrink into the background of the bigger picture. With all the time I spend juggling relationships, work, travel, writing books, booking shows, and looking for a good place to play pinball, I don't have time to fret over some stupid trolls.

I still get idle hands and decide to peek at the comments section from time to time. You can look down at the sewage pit without getting dragged into it. Again, consider the bigger picture. Think of all the difficult things you've overcome in your life and channel that strength. If I could survive Catholic school and grad school, I can survive YouTube. I have been mistreated by real-life people with real-life power, and I still managed to pull through. You think I'm going to worry over some faceless Internet nobodies? The only power they have is the power we give them.

## Fuck 'em

In case I haven't made it clear, let me summarize my position: fuck the trolls! Say it with me (but make sure there are no kids around): FUCK THE TROLLS! We all have haters in our life, in one way or another. If you have something worth saying, someone else will think it's worth tearing down. This is especially true for women. The biggest peak I ever got in YouTube views—and, consequently, negative comments—happened during the Women's March of 2017. I wondered if there was a correlation. Maybe the public show of feminism frightened a lot of men, and some of them decided to take it out on this stuttering female comedian? I showed my channel metrics to my friend Scott, who is a math professor. When I asked him if the sudden spike in activity could happen randomly on its own, he said, "Well, it's fifteen standard deviations away... so yeah, there's a one-in-a-hundred-billion chance that it could be random." Something was happening that week to drive all the sexist backlash on my channel.

For some people, trolling is a hobby. Not watching sports, not painting model trains, not knitting caps for babies in the hospital. Leaving rude and hateful notes for strangers—THAT is what gives them a sense of purpose. They don't know what else to do with themselves, so they try to discourage the rest of us from doing what we love. Misery loves company. They want us to spend less time pursuing our passions and more time wrestling with them in the sewage.

So whether you're doing makeup tutorials or giving a tour of your doomsday prep bunker, be ready for the insults, the slurs, the awkward compliments, the constructive criticism (yeah, right). Oh, and let's not forget those Russian bots! But most of all, be ready for your own emotional response. You can't control others' behavior, but you control how you engage. And if that doesn't work, just disable the damn comments!

## 18
# Why Everyone Should Be Like Ned, Heather, and Mean Dave

Assholisms. Stuttersplaining. Internet trolls. I've spent a lot of this book talking about annoying, awkward, and outright bad behavior. While I hope you find these stories entertaining and informative, please know that they aren't the full story. For all the attention I give to jerks and clowns, there are countless examples of thoughtful people that pass through the background unnoticed. It's not fair, but bad things are just better at standing out. When you break your leg, do you think about the other 205 bones that aren't broken?

Well forget all that. I'm here to tell you it's only one side of the coin. There are plenty of examples of positive behavior that stand out in my mind. People whose actions and words serve as a guide for the rest of the fluent population. People who overcame an ableist culture and expanded their views beyond mere tolerance. They weren't trying to virtue-signal or get woke points with the Disability Community. They did what felt right for them, my relationship with them, and what the situation called for.

The first person I want to mention is Ned, my former boss at the college where I used to work. With Ned, I could go into his office, shut the door, and proceed to unload as many vulgarities as I needed to express myself. He came from an Irish-Italian family in New York, so he understood the value of the casual f-bomb (his had an especially natural quality). That set the tone for the rest of our relationship: open, accepting, and more laid-back than humanly possible in an administrative office. When I first started stand-up, Ned was one of the few people I felt comfortable telling. When *The King's Speech* was playing in theaters and everyone at our school was flagging me down to announce that they had seen the movie—maybe hoping to exchange their ticket stub for a "World's Greatest Ally" coffee mug— Ned was one of the few people who empathized with my irritation.

Ned was always in my corner, but there is one moment in our friendship that deserves special mention. One year, we had representatives from an accrediting body come to evaluate a program at our school. The evaluators arranged to meet with me, Ned, and the rest of the staff. Once they had us all in the same room, they decided to break the ice with a game of "go around and say your name and what you do." As far as I was concerned, they might as well have broken out a cockroach pie and told everyone to dig in. I can stand in front of hundreds of people to give a presentation or perform stand-up, but when I'm in a situation like this, I get anxious. I was making a first impression on people of authority, and I didn't have a chance to disclose my disability the way I normally would. I couldn't set guidelines or manage expectations. My stuttering would be whatever they chose to make of it.

As the rest of the staff took turns introducing themselves, I contemplated various anti-stutter tactics: minimizing my number of words, constructing sentences to avoid tricky syllables—all just to state my name and job! While there might have been a way to dance around my job title, a name is a name is a name. And my name, as you know, is almost a guaranteed stutter. There was nothing for me to do other than brace for impact.

Just like a comedy show, going up last gave me more time to read my audience. One by one, I watched my coworkers introduce themselves to the bureaucrats. One by one, they were met with formal indifference. One of the evaluators was particularly mean. She carried an air of snobbery and emphasized that we were only "staff" at this college—serfs in her academic feudal system. Based on the way she treated everyone else, I knew my impending stutter would be met with some form of hostility. She was also sitting right next to me, which made the whole experience 9,000 times worse.

Then it was my turn. Sure enough, I stuttered on my name and job title. To be fair, "Director of the Office of Disability Services" is enough to make anyone stutter. The woman scrunched up her nose, as if my voice were an offending odor. There may or may not have been an eye roll; my memory is fuzzy on that detail. All I can say is that she made a face. Not just any face—THE Face. People who stutter are very familiar with The Face and its many variations, which can range from "smug smirk" to "patronizing concern." This woman had chosen the arrogant "what the fuck is going on" variety.

I spent the rest of the day trying to shrug off The Face and focus on my work, but it kept eating at me. On Friday, the evaluators sent in their report. Our school did really well! One of them even remarked on the quality of access for students with disabilities (score one for Nina!). The one and only complaint came from (surprise) the woman sitting next to me. Her complaint? A stain on the carpet. Ned and I had a good laugh about that one. Really? The fucking carpet?!

After a bit of joking, I told Ned about the face she had given me during our meeting.

"They looked at me funny," is one of those complaints that people like to dismiss. Common responses include, "I didn't see anything," "You're reading too much into it," and "Are you sure?" Ned said none of these things.

Instead, he said, "Yeah, I noticed that too."

I have never been more grateful to be able to swear in front of my boss!

"Do you want me to say something to her?" Ned offered.

I was floored. Despite the obvious power she held over him, he was willing to call this woman out. Can you imagine a more awkward conversation? "Why did you give a weird look to my stuttering counselor for disabled students?" I told him that wouldn't be necessary, but I let him know how much it meant to me.

This is why everyone should be like Ned. Being like Ned means being willing to stick your neck out for someone else. It means listening to them and acknowledging their experience (f-bombs optional). The fact that Ned validated my account of The Face was enough for me to let it go. It's not easy to imagine life in someone else's shoes, and with stutterers being a one-percent minority, people rarely consider things from our perspective. When someone is willing to make that cognitive leap, I feel incredibly fortunate to have them in my life. Thank you, Ned!

## Mean Dave

Mean Dave is actually a pretty nice guy. Should I explain his name? Nah, just know that it's a contradiction.

Dave is a comedian/cartoonist/heavy metal musician who describes his appearance as a combination of "Jesus, Charles Manson, and Mexican Silent Bob, A.K.A. Roberto de Silencio." He is one of my best friends in life and comedy. He is also an active member of Narcotics Anonymous (five years clean as of this writing). Between his experience with addiction and my experience with disability, we have an easy time relating to each other. He belongs to an NA chapter and I belong to an NSA chapter. We both know what it's like to be deemed defective by society. We both know what it's like to rediscover yourself with support from a specialized community.

When I got married, Dave was one of my bridesmaids—the luckiest bridesmaid ever, since he didn't have to go to the bridal shower and endure any clothespin games (there weren't any, but it was a close call). When I premiered my one-person show, "Going Beyond Inspiration," Dave was my warm-up act. When I decided to write a children's book about learning disabilities (shameless plug alert: *Once Upon an Accommodation*, available on Amazon!), Dave was my creative partner and illustrator. Even now, as I write this book, Dave is helping me edit! Every page of manuscript is covered in notes that we send back and forth to each other. Here's a little gem from the last paragraph:

**Note from Nina:**
Dave, can you fill in how many years you have been clean? Also I assume you are ok with me telling people about your recovery, but let me know if you aren't.

**Note from Dave:**
Sure thing. If you pay me extra, I'll clean out the garbage can you call your car too.

Dave knows all about the inside of my car because we've spent hundreds of hours in it, driving to shows up and down California. We are comedy brothers/sisters in arms. If we're at a show and someone says something dickheaded about my stuttering, Dave has my back. Sometimes he speaks up. Other times we just exchange glances, with Dave saying something like, "I guess it's gonna be one of *those* nights." Just knowing I have someone in my corner is often enough. Other times it gets more involved.

One time we were in Livermore, performing on a show that Dave puts on every Thursday. When the show was over, we stuck around to hang out with the other comics. One of them decided to have a personal conversation about my stuttering in front of the whole group, because that's fun, right?

He said, "Nina, dude. At first I thought you were faking the whole stutter thing. But then you stuttered for real when you talked to me off stage, and I was like, 'Oh, I must make her uncomfortable because now she's stuttering.' But then you didn't stutter another time and I was like, 'Oh, Nina must be more comfortable with me now.'"

Before I had a chance to react, Dave proceeded to give this guy the rundown on how stuttering actually works. It was nice not to be the person explaining for once! Instead, I got to sit back and enjoy watching Dave try to explain neuroscience to a drunk comedian who didn't care. No response required from me. I didn't even have to look annoyed, because Dave did that for me too. He knew exactly when and how to involve himself, without making it about himself.

God knows I've been guilty of making it about me. Like when I got angry on behalf of my friend Steve. Steve Danner is part of the Comedians With Disabilities Act. In 2011, we went to Seattle to audition for NBC's *Stand Up For Diversity*. As we travelled together, I got a front row seat to the constant staring that Steve has to endure as a Little Person. Stares at the gas station. Stares at the restaurant. Stares at the gift shop. This may have been influenced by him wearing a T-shirt that read, "Keep staring at me... I might do a trick." But still! It was too much.

Steve had dealt with stares his whole life and was able to make light of it. He was used to it. I was not. The staring was beyond anything I ever imagined. The invasion of privacy, the disregard for norms and personal boundaries—it pissed me off! I began to channel my anger into staring back at them.

"You know, Steve," I would say, loud enough for everyone to hear, "I enjoy staring at people who stare at you!"

I made the wrong call. I was escalating a situation where Steve himself wasn't even angry. I never asked him how he felt, or how I should support him. Instead, I took it upon myself to create a scene. I was making it all about me! Yuh, no! That's not being an ally!

Mean Dave has never made it about himself. When he dealt with that guy in Livermore, he wasn't patronizing, paternalistic, or self-aggrandizing. Also, unlike me in the case of Steve, Dave wasn't inventing his own response. He had seen me give the same lecture so many times, he figured he might as well give me a break and recite it himself. He took one for the team and modeled how to think and talk about stuttering in front of our peers.

**Note from Dave:**
FUCKING A RIGHT, I DID!

# Heather

Heather is another one of my best friends. She was also a bridesmaid at my wedding—the only one who doesn't qualify for coverage under the Americans with Disabilities Act: Jody has cerebral palsy, Gina stutters, and Dave qualifies as a recovering addict. I met Heather doing stand-up, when she started around the same time as me and Dave. Luckily for her, she lost the comedy bug after a few years and no longer drives hundreds of miles a week chasing laughs from drunks. She still expresses herself as a writer, which is far more fuel-efficient and less likely to result in heckling.

Heather plays a very specific role in my life. When I find myself in an uncomfortable situation, I look to her for a level-headed assessment. When I got upset after a meeting where I stuttered and everyone started yelling out guesses to my next word, *Price is Right* style, I called Heather to see if I was overreacting. When I asked to be on a political-themed show and the booker wrote back, "Oh, you do political material?" I showed the message to Heather. She helped me process my feelings and figure out if I was reading the message correctly. I thought this person knew me well enough to know that my opening joke quotes a civil rights law, not to mention all my other bits about disability which qualify as "political." I was hurt. Heather helped me unpack the situation and form an appropriate response.

Heather is able to empathize and be objective at the same time. Her listening skills are practically a superpower. She allows room for me to decompress and doesn't take it personally when I say something like, "These frickin' able-bodied-fluent shitheads don't know what they're talking about, etc." She doesn't say, "We're not all bad" or "Not all fluent people . . ." I can blow off steam and trust that she won't martyr herself in the name of people who don't stutter. When helping me navigate a tricky situation, she rarely says, "Are you sure about that?" Instead of casting doubt with questions, she answers questions about my doubts. By simply letting me talk, she is able to evaluate the situation and give me an honest appraisal. She has demonstrated her gift for empathy so many times that I believe her when she says I'm overreacting. You really have to be close with someone to trust their instincts over your own emotional response, and Heather provides that closeness.

Everyone should have a Heather in their life. And everyone should be like Heather!

The stories in this chapter are all stories of personal relationships. How you support people with disabilities depends on your relationship with them. Mean Dave is able to joke about my stuttering because we know each other in the context of comedy and share an emotional trust built up over several years. When he jokes, "What can I say about Nina that wouldn't take her longer to say about herself?" I know that it's coming from a place of love. I wouldn't consider it appropriate behavior from someone like a boss or coworker (not even a boss like Ned). Everyone has a different role. When you befriend a person who stutters, you will gradually learn your role in their life. Let it happen naturally, and don't press them for answers. I try to educate people about stuttering whenever it seems productive, but that is a donation of my time and energy to something I care about. No one is required to provide a free sensitivity workshop.

That doesn't mean there aren't resources out there. Elizabeth Wislar and Hope Gerlach have created a wonderful online guide, *How to Be a Fluent Ally to People Who Stutter.*[1] The guide provides simple, straightforward advice like "Don't be afraid to ask if you don't know how to help" and "Allies take responsibility for participating in their own education about stuttering." Plus, the drawings are adorable!

Every day presents a new opportunity to help others. Whether you are supporting friends, family, or even a stranger, you have the ability to make a difference in someone's life. Make it a positive difference.

# 19
# Transforming The Iceberg

I have very little control over my stutter. I wouldn't even call it control; it's more like I have to bargain with it. "Hey Nina's Stutter, if I put on my 'business voice' and totally not sound like myself, will you let me get through this one phone call with a stranger?" "If I avoid this word or that word, will you at least stay out of my next sentence?" I get exhausted just thinking about it. If I planned my day around Nina's Stutter, there wouldn't be time for anything else. Life is short, and I'm not going to waste it trying to control what I can't control.

Stuttering is one of the few constants in my life. My hair has changed, my clothes have changed, my address has changed—but Nina's Stutter is here to stay. It has never changed, and it probably never will. But the way I think and feel about it has changed.

I used to hate Nina's Stutter. I was ashamed of it. I devoted the best parts of my youth to fighting it, instead of doing what made me feel happy and productive. The more I missed out on life, the more I blamed Nina's Stutter, doubling down my efforts to kill it. If only I were fluent, everything else would fall into place! I could speak freely. I could have boys ask me to prom. I could even follow my dreams and be a stand-up comic. All I had to do was stop stuttering!

When I write it down, it seems so ridiculous. How can some pauses and a few extra syllables take control of a person's entire life?

That question became a point of focus for Joseph Sheehan, a clinical researcher and psychologist. Throughout his career, he observed that stuttering was typically more disruptive to a person's emotional wellbeing than it was to their actual speech. In *Stuttering: Research and Therapy* (1970), Sheehan writes that "stuttering is like an iceberg, with only a small part above the waterline and a much bigger part below." According to Sheehan, what most people think of as "stuttering" is only the tip of iceberg—the outwardly observable symptoms on the surface. But the emotional baggage that comes with it—the invisible pain underneath—that's where the bulk of the ice really is. Sheehan organized these murky, underwater emotions into seven categories: fear, denial, shame, anxiety, isolation, guilt, and hopelessness. According to Sheehan, as the stutterer resolves these issues, the negative emotions begin to "evaporate." This in turn causes the "waterline" to lower, until, finally, all that remains is the physical stutter.

*The iceberg on the left depicts the traditional Sheehan iceberg with the negative feelings people have about their stutter. The right side offers an alternative way to think about stuttering. Image drawn by Jesse Elias.*

Sheehan's book became highly influential in its field. The iceberg theory advanced a more holistic view of stuttering, inspiring professionals to consider more than just the sounds coming out of a person's mouth. It also helped me think about my own experience. I know all about those emotions below the water. I have felt guilty for making people wait through a stalled sentence. I have felt isolated, especially before discovering the stuttering community. But most of all, I have felt shame, simply for speaking the way that I speak.

Although it provides a useful framework, I don't think Sheehan's Iceberg presents the full picture. Sure, it explains the negative things we feel, but what about the other emotions? Just like everyone else, the life of a stutterer is filled with ups and downs, victories and defeats, good times and bad times. Even if your overall situation doesn't change, things might look better or worse on a given day depending what side of the bed you wake up on. It's all a matter of perspective.

If you've ever lain on the grass and looked up at the clouds, you know how easily perspective can change. One minute this cloud looks like a dragon; the next minute it looks like a bunny rabbit. Unless El Niño is brewing up an apocalyptic tornado, that cloud probably hasn't changed much in the last sixty seconds. Instead, you let your eyes wander, reoriented your perspective, and unknowingly formed a different mental picture of the same thing.

If it can be done with literal clouds, then it can be done with metaphorical icebergs. Stuttering doesn't have to be a bad experience if we change our perspective. Before I found the stuttering community, my perspective was all negative. I was isolated, ashamed, and everything else Sheehan packs into that sad popsicle. But when I found the National Stuttering Project during that summer in high school, something changed. I was no longer isolated—I had found a community. I was no longer ashamed. Maybe even... proud?

Sheehan writes about negative emotions evaporating until only a stutter remains. I disagree. When bad feelings subside, other feelings have to take their place. We don't refer to happiness as "not sadness," or confidence as "not embarrassment." The negative emotions in Sheehan's Iceberg all have positive equivalents. I propose that we can do more than simply make the bad feelings go away; we have the power to transform fear, shame, anxiety, isolation, denial, guilt, and hopelessness into feelings of courage, pride, comfort, community, acceptance, kindness, and hope.

So how do we do that? Although the negative emotions in Sheehan's Iceberg are common to the stuttering experience, they are common because we live in a society that treats people with disabilities as substandard. But we don't have to buy into it. All the weird looks we get in public, all the shitty images we see in the media, all the lowered expectations that people project onto us—they can all be thrown out and replaced with something better. Instead of struggling to conform to the ideals of a culture that makes us feel deficient, we can cultivate our own perspective and learn to love ourselves as we are. Every person who stutters has the responsibility to create their own iceberg—one that reflects their best possible self.

How we are perceived is largely influenced by how we perceive ourselves. When I began to accept my stutter, so did the people around me. Friends and family stopped offering advice on how to improve my fluency. People stopped thinking of me as a weirdo (at least after high school). Obviously there is a limit to how much self-perception can determine the views of others: I can't force an asshole to stop being an asshole, as we've seen countless times in this book. But I can determine my own worth and decide which assholes are beneath me. I can share my values with the world, doing what I can to sway us from that asshole culture toward something more loving and equitable.

Promoting stuttering acceptance has been one of my greatest missions in life. Everyone who interacts with us, thinks about us, studies us, works with us, produces movies and TV shows about us, reports on us—they all have stuttering icebergs too! Just like Sheehan's model, the strange and shitty ways they treat us are just the tip of the iceberg, stemming from murky emotions beneath the surface. If we are ever going to overcome discrimination, we have to address the emotional baggage of these people as well. It's not going to be easy. It's hard enough to understand my own feelings toward stuttering, much less model them for others! All I can do is put myself in front of the public and try my best—in bars and comedy clubs, on college campuses, in online videos and social media, and now in this book. Changing minds isn't easy, but I'll take that over trying to change who I am.

# 20
# Creating Utopia

Every time I walk into a stuttering conference, it feels like I'm entering a utopia. A place where I can speak freely without fear of being interrupted. Where, if someone were to interrupt me, another person would step in and say, "Wait for her to finish!" In Stuttering Utopia, we don't have to fight for space to express ourselves. We can chat with strangers in hallways and elevators without fear of getting looks or awkward comments. Nobody makes The Face. I never have to justify my existence to strangers. I can talk in my own voice and expect to be treated like everyone else.

I imagine that last sentence describes any day of the week for most fluent people. But if you go through life watching people flinch when you speak, the difference is dramatic. With all the stigmas and barriers stripped away, you gain a deeper understanding of yourself. You can finally see the world without looking through the distorted lens of ableism. You can shed the fears and the masks and step into your most authentic self.

But then, at the end of every conference, there's always that comedown of having to leave our little utopia and return to that bigger, less-than-perfect world out there. But I always take something back with me. I'm not talking about T-shirts, or water bottles, although

I love those things too. It's the memories they represent. You can't capture the beauty of Yellowstone in a magnet from the gift shop, but every time I see it on my fridge, it makes me smile. I'm reminded of the incredible things I felt when I was there. That's how it is with a stuttering conference: the beauty is in the feelings that stay with you afterward. I always come back with new insights and revelations—about myself, about the world... about everything.

The 2009 NSA conference helped me realize what was missing from my own life. "Oh, you mean I can expect people to shut up while I speak?" No one ever tells you that until you've been exposed to a stutter-centric community. At the 2016 conference, I started thinking about what was missing from the rest of the world. I thought of all the people who couldn't attend the conference: because they didn't know about it; because they couldn't afford it; because they were shy, ashamed, or afraid. I realized that Stuttering Utopia isn't big enough. We need to include more than just a few thousand people for one week in one hotel in one part of the world; we have to go out and make it a reality for everyone else.

For some people, commonality only feels achievable in a specific environment. It might be a stuttering conference, a pride parade, or a Star Trek convention—in each example, people wait all year for a special gathering because it gives them a place where they can feel like themselves. But a few days out of a whole year isn't enough. We need to figure out how to recreate that experience in the other 99% of our lives.

When I came home from the 2009 conference, I realized that Stuttering Utopia and the "real world" don't have to be two different things. The conference was over, but what it represented to me—community, dignity, the ability to engage the world on my own terms—those things could be integrated into my everyday life. I could build my own utopia, as long as I was willing to make tough choices and fight for them. For me, this meant breaking up with my long term boyfriend and pushing myself to finally enter the world of stand-up comedy. I stopped denying myself a voice out of fear of inconveniencing others. I became upfront about my dysfluency, my needs, and my desires. Maybe Stuttering Utopia is an unattainable ideal, but pursuing it has made my life so much better.

You can create a personal, portable version of your own utopia. But only you can do it. No one else is going to make it happen. The first step is figuring out what you want. When you find yourself in that utopian space, pay attention to what is going on and how it makes you feel. Identify the parts that make you happy and break them down to their core ideas. Once you've picked out these magical idea seeds, you need to find a way to make them grow in your own backyard. The things we get from a conference can be had from the rest of the world, but you have to speak up and ask for it. You have to be willing to make changes in your life. You might even have to fight for social change. What are the changes that need to happen for you? For your family? For your friends? For everyone else?

Building your own utopia is hard. Trying to extend that utopia to the rest of society is even harder. People are amazed when I tell them about my mission to promote stuttering acceptance. They think of me like Don Quixote and the windmill, wondering how I can devote my time to something they view as hopeless and silly. You can bet they wouldn't bat a fluent eyelash if I told them I was dedicating the same amount of time to "fixing" my stutter And that shows exactly why our work needs to continue.

Our work . . . what does that mean? It means promoting realistic images of stuttering to counter misrepresentation in the media. It means funding research that will measure and address discrimination in personal and professional environments. It means reaching out to the people who have never been to a stuttering conference and removing barriers to access. It means identifying not only as stutterers, but every aspect of ourselves, so that issues of gender, sexual orientation, race, culture, and disability and their intersection with stuttering can be understood and celebrated. It means teaching law enforcement, educators, and employers how to interact with people who stutter, and teaching people who stutter to know their rights. It means challenging speech pathologists, social workers, psychotherapists, and other professionals to advocate for stuttering rights and to use their influence not simply to treat our speech, but to treat the prejudices of society. These are just a few of my ideas; I encourage you to develop your own ways of making the world a more stutter-friendly and loving place!

Of the many, many things I have learned from the Disability Community, one of the most important is this: the issues that impact people with disabilities impact everyone. When you address those issues, there is a ripple effect that benefits everybody. The ramp that is added to a building for wheelchair access makes that building better for everyone. By turning our Stuttering Utopia outward to include the world around us, we can change everyone's lives for the better.

# Notes

## CHAPTER 1:

1. Edith Ann was eventually autographed by her namesake, when I went with my parents and Godmother Carolyn to see Lily Tomlin perform in Berkeley.

2. I eventually found my way back to Dorsey's Locker eighteen years later, and to this day it is still one of my favorite mics. I even headlined there one night and shared this story. That's right, for one night at Dorsey's this bitch was Eddie Murphy.

## CHAPTER 3:

1. The scientific term is "verbal automaticity."

2. I am happy to report that Sara now works as a teacher in San Jose, where many more children can benefit from her kindness and support.

## CHAPTER 4:

1. Why a person who stutters would give herself a stage name with two Ms, I have no idea. Perhaps Marilyn was more of a C and G-word type of stutterer?

## CHAPTER 5:

1. This was during the very, very, small window of time when Stuttering John was actually cute. Yes, I am rating him on his looks. Consider it payback for a show where all the guys ranked women on their hotness. How does it feel, fellas?

2. I recently learned that the love between Howard and John eventually became strained and fizzled out, as revealed in John's tell-all book, *Easy For You to Say*.

## CHAPTER 6:

1. Years later, after volunteering in a third grade classroom, it dawned on me that I hate teaching reading. Explaining what letters sound like is the exact place where my learning disability manifests, and my phonemic awareness sucks. If I became a third grade teacher, my class would be filled with kids who felt good about themselves, appreciated each other's differences, and didn't know how to read! Needless to say, I turned my vocational interests elsewhere.

## CHAPTER 9:

1. Brainwash isn't just a fun name for a place where you wash your clothes. It's a reference to the newspaper heiress Patty Hearst, who was held captive by the Symbionese Liberation Army in a basement across the street. They brainwashed her into joining their army and robbing a bank in 1974. She spent two years in prison. Bill Clinton pardoned her in 2001. Kind of a heavy legacy to hang on your wacky laundromat/cafe/performance space.

2. The Madonna Inn is a themed hotel that looks like it was cobbled together from different parts of Disneyland. The rooms have showers that look like caves. Shag carpet and plastic grapes are everywhere. The men's urinal is a waterfall that flushes away the pee. If you are going through San Luis Obispo on Highway 101,

you should really stop there to use the bathroom. On any given day you'll see bemused women snapping pictures of the water-fall urinal. It could very well be the most Italian/tacky place in California.

## CHAPTER 12:

1. You can see the sketches on Comedy Central's website (if you don't mind sitting through the stupid Geico ads).

2. When I told my friend Heather that Dave Chappelle compared me to the first five minutes of *Do The Right Thing*, she thought he was talking about the opening credits where Rosie Perez does her kickass dance to "Fight the Power." As I always say, everyone should have a Heather in their life!

## CHAPTER 18:

1. http://isad.isastutter.org/isad-2017/papers-presented-by/creative-expression/how-to-be-a-fluent-ally-to-people-who-stutter-an-illustrated-guide/

# Resources for the Stuttering Community

There are many organizations that help people who stutter. This is a list of all the ones mentioned in this book, plus some others that I want people to know about. While there are organizations that focus on achieving fluency, I have chosen not to include them here. This is a list of organizations that promote community and self-acceptance for the stuttering population.

## Resources in the United States

National Stuttering Association (formerly the National Stuttering Project): The NSA changed my life and continues to change my life, as it has for so many others. The NSA offers regional support groups across the United States and hosts a massive conference every year in the first week of July. They provide services for people of all ages, including special programming for young adults at their annual conference. The NSA also provides education to speech and language professionals through conference symposiums and workshops.

www.westutter.org

FRIENDS (who stutter):  FRIENDS helps young people who stutter, their families, and the professionals who serve them. It has a yearly conference as well as regional events.

https://www.friendswhostutter.org:

Passing Twice:  Passing Twice is a community of LGBTQ people who stutter and their allies.  It holds workshops at stuttering conferences and provides an informal network through its quarterly newsletter, e-mail list, and annual mailing list.

www.passingtwice.org

American Institute for Stuttering: AIS serves people who stutter in a therapeutic capacity. It focuses on quality of life rather than fluency. It offers tele-therapy as well as scholarships for its services.

www.stutteringtreatment.org

SAY (The Stuttering Association of the Young): SAY helps children and teens who stutter with summer camps, after school programs, and other youth-oriented services. It empowers children who stutter by encouraging them to embrace their voice.

www.say.org

The Stuttering Foundation: The Stuttering Foundation is an organization that focuses on educating the public as well as speech and language therapists. The foundation put together an awesome project in response to Kylie Simmons being detained at the Atlanta airport after stuttering in customs (the officials thought her stuttering was suspicious). Kylie and The Stuttering Foundation worked together to develop an "I Stutter" card for presenting to authority figures in difficult situations. I always carry one in my wallet!

www.StutteringHelp.org

## International Resources

International Stuttering Association (ISA): The International Stuttering Association is made up of national groups with the aim of helping others understand stuttering.

Irish Stammering Association (also ISA): The Irish Stammering Association offers support groups, summer camps for kids, and many other services across Ireland. It also holds a conference once a year around International Stuttering (AKA Stammering) Awareness Day. Fun fact: I once performed with two other stammering comedians on a comedy show produced by ISA!

    https://stammeringireland.ie

The Indian Stammering Association (TISA): TISA holds conferences and provides services in many different Indian languages. Speaking of Indian languages, TISA once marched through the streets carrying a banner that read "Haklao Magar Pyaar," which translates to "Stammer With Love." I love that!

    http://stammer.in

British Stammering Association: BSA educates, advocates, and creates community for individuals who stammer. Check out their website to learn more about all the great work they do. Also be sure to read the groovy mission statement!

    www.Stammering.org

Canadian Stuttering Association: CSA holds conferences and other community events, supports people who stutter and their families, and educates the public on stuttering.

    www.stutter.ca

## Podcasts:

*Women Who Stutter: Our Stories*: Pam Mertz has interviewed 170 women in 35 countries!

She created the podcast as a space for women to share their unique voices. As Pam says, "Everyone has a story to tell. They just need to be asked."

www.StutterRockStar.com

*StutterTalk: StutterTalk* is the longest running podcast on stuttering, with over 600 shows. Experts in speech and language therapy and other disciplines join host Peter Reitzes to talk about all things stuttering.

www.StutterTalk.com

*Stuttering Is Cool:* As its name implies, *Stuttering is Cool* is a podcast promoting self-acceptance. Daniele Rossi hosts. Daniele is also an artist who creates wonderful cartoons, some of which have been published in his book, *Stuttering is Cool: A Guide to Stuttering in a Fast-Talking World.*

www.StutteringIsCool.com

Make sure to celebrate International Stuttering Awareness Day on October 22nd and National Stuttering Awareness Week (in the United States) in the second week of May!

# Acknowledgments

Jesse Elias definitely gets the first thank you!  Jesse, you had my comedy heart so many years ago at "penis fog."  I am thrilled that one of the most creative people to come out of San Francisco comedy could guide me through the process of writing this book!

Thank you to Mean Dave and Lara Gabrielle Fowler for your constant feedback and edits. Editing the book of someone with dyslexia is quite an undertaking, and your assistance has been invaluable!

Thank you to my husband Ethan for supporting me in dedicating the time and money to this project. This was a self-funded project, so please buy the book for all your friends and family so that Ethan and I can continue to pay our rent!

Thank you to my parents for supporting me through life, comedy, and writing this book. You have endured a lot, especially sitting through all those amateur comedy shows to see me perform. I'll never forget what mom said after a particularly bad lineup at The Improv: "That's not comedy; that's bullshit." Thank you for your love, unconditional support, and letting me say all the things I've said about our family. If anyone gets angry, I'll just say you didn't know about it.

Thank you to all the friends, fellow comedians, comedy bookers, producers, and stutterers who have been part of my story. You guys made it all possible!

Thank you to all the wonderful stuttering organizations out there. I encourage readers to seek them out (turn to page 134)! Thank you to the National Stuttering Association, the Indian Stammering Association, the Irish Stammering Association, and the International Stuttering Association for helping me combine my comedy with advocacy.

I would also like to acknowledge Brooke Warner and everyone at She Writes Press for their assistance with this book. It is such a gift to be able to tell my story without pressure to be an "inspiration." And also to be able to write the word "fuck."

# About the Author

Nina G is a comedian, professional speaker and Disability advocate. She travels the country performing at comedy clubs and colleges and keynoting at conferences. She is part of the comedy troupe The Comedians with Disabilities Act, which brings laughter and awareness to audiences of all ages across the country. Nina lives in Oakland with her husband, Ethan, who is a comedian and educator. Since comedians should never quit their day job, she also works as a counselor for students with disabilities at a California Community College, which she loves almost as much as stand-up comedy. She has contributed to numerous books on stuttering and disability studies, including her own children's book, *Once Upon an Accommodation: A Book About Learning Disabilities*.

To book Nina at your event go to www.ninagcomedian.com

For bonus content go to www.stuttererinterrupted.com

# SELECTED TITLES FROM SHE WRITES PRESS

She Writes Press is an independent publishing company founded to serve women writers everywhere. Visit us at www.shewritespress.com.

*Rethinking Possible: A Memoir of Resilience* by Rebecca Faye Smith Galli. $16.95, 978-1-63152-220-8

After her brother's devastatingly young death tears her world apart, Becky Galli embarks upon a quest to recreate the sense of family she's lost—and learns about healing and the transformational power of love over loss along the way.

*Not a Poster Child: Living Well with a Disability—A Memoir* by Francine Falk-Allen. $16.95, 978-1631523915

Francine Falk-Allen was only three years old when she contracted polio and temporarily lost the ability to stand and walk. Here, she tells the story of how a toddler learned grown-up lessons too soon; a schoolgirl tried her best to be a "normie," on into young adulthood; and a woman finally found her balance, physically and spiritually.

*Not by Accident: Reconstructing a Careless Life* by Samantha Dunn. $16.95, 978-1-63152-832-3

After suffering a nearly fatal riding accident, lifelong klutz Samantha Dunn felt compelled to examine just what it was inside herself—and other people—that invited carelessness and injury.

*This Trip Will Change Your Life: A Shaman's Story of Spirit Evolution* by Jennifer B. Monahan. $16.95, 978-1-63152-111-9

One woman's inspirational story of finding her life purpose and the messages and training she received from the spirit world as she became a shamanic healer.

*Body 2.0: Finding My Edge Through Loss and Mastectomy* by Krista Hammerbacher Haapala

An authentic, inspiring guide to reframing adversity that provides a new perspective on preventative mastectomy, told through the lens of the author's personal experience.